A DEADLY PLAN . . .

"You know you need to get that girl outta your house," Stephanie advised, taking her eyes off the road and turning around for emphasis. " 'Cause she's just manipulating every single one of you."

Then suddenly there was a plan, with specifics that seemed to materialize on their own: They were going to take Stacey outside somewhere where her screams couldn't be heard—and teach her a lesson.

"I know the perfect spot," Tracy said. Behind the Chesterfield County airport, down near where she grew up. A place called Marsh Field . . .

A
FATAL
LIE

A True Story of Betrayal and Murder in the New South

SALLY CHEW

St. Martin's Paperbacks

A FATAL LIE

Copyright © 1999 by Sally Chew.

Cover photograph of house © *Richmond Times Dispatch*. Used with permission. Mug shots by Chesterfield County Police.

ISBN: 0-312-97014-5

Printed in the United States of America

St. Martin's Paperbacks edition/September 1999

10 9 8 7 6 5 4 3 2 1

FOR MY FATHER

ACKNOWLEDGMENTS

Despite my Southern roots, I'm a Yankee outsider in Virginia. You wouldn't know it, though, from the warmth and generosity I enjoyed during the research for this book—or maybe that's the point about Southerners.

Alan Cooper, a wise observer of the criminal justice system, and human behavior too, also happens to be a reporter for the *Richmond Times–Dispatch*. His steady guidance and encyclopedic knowledge were invaluable to me. Mark Bowes and Tom Campbell at the same newspaper were helpful as well.

Among the many others who shared their expertise were Ralph White of the James River Park System and members of the Sexual Minorities Student Alliance at Virginia Commonwealth University. I also want to thank Elizabeth Bernhard, Director of the Chesterfield County Victim Witness Protection Program; Deborah Marlowe, Director of Community Relations for the Chesterfield County Schools; and the Chesterfield County Police Department, especially the detectives who appear in these pages.

Tara Slate Donaldson and Rebecca Sams are family now, but I was only supposed to borrow the couch. Instead, they gave me the run of their home and inspired me with gossip and cooking.

Back home in New York, it got even easier. Beth Freeman provided crucial technical help. My agent, Ellen Geiger, and my editor, Charles Spicer, bombarded me with confidence. And Sara and Seth Faison, my mother and stepfather, gave me a place to finish the job in peace, not to mention the kind of support that most people only dream of from their relations.

Finally, I'm indebted to David France and Laura Perry, who very concretely helped me turn this story into a book. Their importance to me as fellows and friends, having by now withstood every other test, could never be matched.

AUTHOR'S NOTE

This book represents my belief about what happened during the summer of 1997 and the events before and since, based on hundreds of interview hours and an exhaustive review of legal documents. Some of the dialogue was reconstructed from personal recollections. The names Marisa, Peter, Will, and Sharon are not those individuals' real names.

When Tracy opened the back door of the car, the ceiling light blinked on, and she had just enough time to see that blood and earth had fully sopped her white corduroy shorts and bare limbs. A red circle bloomed in the right armpit of her t-shirt. She dropped onto the seat, and it was dark again.

Domica arrived next, making four. And everything fell quiet once she was shut in, except for the soft tinkle of alarm bells that repeated out into the night through the open passenger door—Turtle's door. They all stared forward at the glow of headlights on the pines. Where was Turtle?

Tracy and Domica had returned with heaving chests and now their breathing finally slowed. Still, no one spoke, even as Turtle finally waddled out of the dark, lifting slow, swampy sneakers toward the car.

But then they had to know.

"Is she dead?" Tracy asked.

It was a straightforward question, not the test of loyalty between teenage lovers that it might have been—measuring out which one of these two had actually, finally finished off the girl who had gotten between them. The original mission of their night was still lost in the messy efforts of the group.

Domica, whose voice rushed in now without waiting for Turtle's response, was even more focused on results.

"Maybe we should go back and make sure she's dead," Domica suggested.

Turtle was quite clear, though: "No," she said. "I know she's dead. When I was walkin' away I picked up a stick, and I went back and stabbed it in her."

She turned to Stephanie then, stiff and sweating behind the steering wheel. "Let's just fucking go," Turtle told her.

The car growled into reverse, and Turtle looked into the black air outside her window, away from her friends, as if to will herself gone or to end this conversation unmistakably.

Instead, the discussion that followed on the drive up Nash Road took a direct cue from the story of Turtle's skillfully flourished stick. The others wanted to tell their stories, too.

Perhaps they were genuinely marveling at how difficult it had been to squeeze the life out of a young body without the benefit of decent weapons. None of them had ever done this before.

But what it sounded like—certainly to Stephanie and to Dana, neither of whom had actually walked down that logging road and stood over Stacey's body—was bragging, pure and simple. They were proud of what they had done, about the obstacles they had overcome.

"Holy shit," Tracy said. "Her neck wouldn't break."

"I know, man. What the fuck?" agreed Domica.

"I fucking slit her throat," Tracy continued, and in announcing that, she remembered the power of the moment— the flash of joy. She was still too much a part of this team not to tell the others about it.

"It felt good," she told them.

Domica's turn came next. And she was exhilarated too, reeling as she was from her first-ever experience of being on top in a beating. It seemed nothing less than miraculous that her frantic, unchanneled rage had helped end Stacey's life.

There was something brave about it, and right now, with the blood on her body still indistinguishable from the mud, she wanted to remember exactly how it had been.

"I was stabbing her," she said. "I wanted her fucking heart."

PROLOGUE

In Richmond, Virginia, during the week of Stacey Hanna's murder, somebody driving a bronze-colored Cadillac pulled up alongside Harold M. Marsh, an esteemed local attorney stuck in traffic at a busy intersection, and shot him to death. Also, the Ethyl Corporation flattened eight Victorian homes in Oregon Hill, the city's oldest neighborhood, after a long fight in court. And 35,000 boys swarmed into the area from around the world for a National Scout Jamboree.

In the dank, grouchy heat of late July, these were crushing developments for some Richmonders. The Marsh case especially. His civic contributions were itemized again and again, a $25,000 reward was posted for leads to his killer, and the victim's brother, a state senator, took the occasion to raise a ruckus about gun control in the General Assembly building downtown.

But then folks cooled off, their attentions moved on. In Richmond, the Capital of the Confederacy during the Civil War, tens of thousands of soldiers are buried around town as a reminder of that defeat. It's *traditional* to move on. As long as everything stays in its place. The Boy Scouts way out at the Army post. And the murders in the city.

In the summer of 1997, more people resided in suburban Chesterfield County, the tobacco-scented corridor of the city's "South Side," than in Richmond proper. But it was mostly robberies that called police to the small towns and woodland homes there. And it was mostly middle-class Baptist families, very happy to keep the metropolis at arm's length, who phoned. Gang murders and lesbian love triangles were not in their place.

Chesterfield County Detective Dave Zeheb had seen dead people before when he was called away from Sunday night television on July 27th to the water-logged, slashed body of a youthful woman, the right side of her head resting on folded arms. But as the details emerged, Detective Zeheb found this case puzzling—"one of a kind," he said.

One of a kind even in the bigger, national picture of teenage murders at the time. Because the quick slam of a bullet wasn't to blame. In this case, the killers had been a long time at it. The coroner counted 65 shallow cuts, one of them through the girl's trachea and 21 crowded into the same frayed place above her heart.

Stacey Hanna's body, naked but for red bikini underwear, had also been pummeled and dragged. Her lungs were tight pouches of sandy liquid, and from the fine, furry layer of silt on her skin, police deduced that a pool of sandy water had dropped slowly around her in the 18 or 20 hours that she lay undiscovered. Surely that puddle had been enough to drown her, if the loss of blood hadn't taken her first.

Among the items on the medical examiner's initial list of unexplained marks were a large, bluish bruise on her left hand, just above the thumb—it looked like one of those home tattoos—and a sweeping pattern of slashes along the front of her right leg that resembled the letters "L-I-A-R." Either this last wound was a freakish coincidence of lines, or it was one of the most direct announcements of a victim's offense that the examiner's office had ever seen.

There was less of a mystery about who was responsible for all of this. Even before Detective Zeheb came upon the raw sight in the woods, he had his killers. As daytime television picked up the scent on Monday, Richmonders learned the names of four teenage girls who had been raised in their very midst, three in the county itself. And right away they could see that the four had come to no good in the edgy urban area they were calling home, 15 miles directly to the north of that muddy spot.

For some South Side people, Stacey Hanna's murder was the first window on a world that they had already imagined for the insolent students and eyesore slackers of the city's Carytown district. Whether or not it had come to their attention that Richmond was becoming one of the gayest areas in the South, it wasn't news that the colleges up there attracted freaks and out-of-towners. Of course a band of shaved-headed lesbians—no school, no grownups—would thrive there. And kill? Well, maybe.

It was also a natural leap of logic for the county's narrower minds to match the evil of the crime with the mysterious homosexual love story that emerged. Who remembered a murder this gruesome, and who knew lesbians? Accounts hinted that the victim had crossed some underground rule, triggered some insanity that heterosexuals shouldn't bother trying to understand.

Stacey's attackers offered not a single sympathetic scrap for watchers of local WTVR-TV or readers of the *Richmond Times–Dispatch*. Domica Winckler told Detective Rick Mormando, "It was just one of those times . . . when somebody had to die," and he passed that on. Parallels with a 1992 killing involving a group of lesbians in New Albany, Indiana, suggested some kind of sick trend.

Of course, the opposite was true: The lesbian twist was so interesting because it was so rare. Murderesses of any sexual persuasion would have had Richmonders craning their necks. But love this dark between women was unfathomable.

Four criminal trials tied up the second floor of the Chesterfield County Courthouse with the case through the winter and spring of 1998. And it didn't take much to demonstrate that the girls who killed Stacey Hanna were damaged goods. There had been sexual abuse, poverty, suicide attempts, and all manner of punishments at home and at school for liking other girls *that way*.

Evidence like that could take jurors either way on a verdict—not to mention the death penalty. Who knew where the line between sinful and sympathetic might be drawn?

The other questions were even harder to answer: What did Stacey Hanna do wrong? Was there "domestic violence'' here that the usual radar failed to pick up? Why couldn't Turtle Tibbs, Tracy Bitner, Domica Winckler, and Stephanie Cull just move on, cool off?

Not even the level-headed elders in the girls' lives, watching their backs, expecting better days ahead, saw the deadliness of this romantic tangle. But then, neither did the killers themselves. Nobody was more surprised.

CAST OF CHARACTERS

Kelley - "Turtle"
Tracy - the girlfriend
Domica - the neighbor
Stephanie - the driver
Stacey - the new girl
Dana - the witness
Robyn - "Dad"
Sandy - Tracy's other woman
Claire - Stephanie's girlfriend

PART ONE

210 South Belmont Avenue

FOXFIRE NEVER LOOKS BACK! was one of our secret proverbs. Also FOXFIRE BURNS & BURNS and FOXFIRE NEVER SAYS SORRY! but such pertained to regret and remorse and guilt and sin and repentance such as weaker people might feel, not to memory. And such predated, I guess I should state clearly, the nightmare events of FOXFIRE's final days of May–June 1956 which I believe no one of us did not regret.

For FOXFIRE was a true outlaw gang, yes . . .

But FOXFIRE was a true blood-sisterhood, our bond forged in loyalty, fidelity, trust, love.

—from Foxfire: Confessions of a Girl Gang,
by Joyce Carol Oates

1:

With all the bright white columns and lovingly mortared red brick walls, Richmond could be Colonial Williamsburg or even Washington, D.C. Same Thomas Jefferson aesthetic, same lush overhang of flowering trees—an American-heritage picture postcard at every turn.

Other centuries have been just as good to Richmond, though, and sometimes the Old South seems to defer. In the city's Fan District, for example, the red bricks are underfoot. The houses themselves are yellow or blue or gray, with shady porches and two-tone Victorian gingerbread.

The Fan, like the Carytown district to its west, belongs to the so-called New South, in love with the past and obsessively modern at the same time. Politics, pedigrees, and generations are supposed to mix as happily here as the architecture.

The neighborhood is named for the way the avenues slant gently away from each other. It's green and quiet along the edges, with one-way streets and quaint corner cafés. An occasional art gallery is open only on Saturdays.

Then it starts to get urban and busy down near the "handle" of the Fan, at the approach to VCU—Virginia Commonwealth University. Right away you hear music and smell coffee. The front yards are rattier. At the intersection of West Grace and North Harrison Streets, a Kurt Cobain lookalike walks by. A pack of teenage girls, unwrapping candy and smoking cigarettes at the same time, wear jeans that fold into the sidewalk. This is the cosmopolitan soul of the city, Richmond's pierced nipple.

*　　*　　*

Eighteen-year-old Robyn Thirkill, a reluctant VCU fresh-
man, crossed that corner for the first time on a hot day in
the middle of September 1993, looking not at all like the
daughter of the suburbs that she was. First you realized that
the black guy in the backwards black baseball cap was not,
in fact, a guy. Then you saw the tattoos.

Robyn looped back at Goshen Street and for a second
time passed a squat, smiling white girl in shorts, the sleeves
of her t-shirt rolled up over wide, solid arms. The girl was
watching the sidewalk traffic outside the Grace Street Cin-
emas.

"Hey," she said, and Robyn stopped. They were squint-
ing at each other because the sun was so bright, and this
caused the girl's big green eyes to twinkle mischievously.

"Whassup?" Robyn inquired.

The answer was just that the girl was thinking of catching
a show and did Robyn want to come too? She wedged the
fingers of her right hand into a tight front pocket, where a
chain hooked her belt loop, fell long and loose across her
thigh, and disappeared around back. She glanced down
Grace Street, and Robyn could see that her medium-brown
hair, a short fringe over an otherwise shaved scalp, wound
down into a small braided tail in the back.

"Sure," came Robyn's reply.

Even at 14—she told Robyn 16—Turtle Tibbs was always collecting strangers, bringing somebody back from the
mall, the record store, the river. Future best friends or not,
the method was the same.

"We went out on one date," Robyn would recall later,
"and decided that that was really gross of us to date each
other. We've been like brothers, pals, ever since. Nothing's
ever happened between us, we're just butch pals."

Butch, of course, being more than Robyn's heavy black
boots or the slow-motion swagger that helped earn Turtle
her name. "We were chivalrous and we were gentle dykes
and we were tough," Robyn would try to explain.

* * *

On the surface, these two had little else in common. Turtle chatted up sweethearts and shop merchants with equal verve and hadn't been to school since she was 12; Robyn was charming too, but she presided with understatement and reserve—and one level eye on the mess that Turtle was generally making. Her street smarts were more a matter of natural style than rough upbringing.

It was love for each other's company that sent them prowling the city as a team. They would head out late on a Friday to hear a local band at the Flood Zone or 6th Street Marketplace or down to the James River to confer on the rocks, Robyn with her Winstons and Turtle dipping a bag of chewing tobacco. Railroad trestles bisect the north bank and tower over the beach. There was a rope up there and you could swing out over the agitated brown water, let it slip through your fingers, and fight the current.

Another destination was Belle Isle, 60 wooded acres in the middle of the James where 20,000 Yankee prisoners are supposed to have festered during the Civil War. Sometimes girlfriends were in tow, sometimes not. It was a short hike by footbridge, a cat's cradle of ramps strung under the traffic on the Robert E. Lee Bridge and haunted at all hours by the hollow echo of bouncing tires.

All this play left no time for school, and Robyn dropped out when the semester ended in December. By now she knew: It was Richmond The City she was after. She got her tongue pierced and spent more time in her pickup. Pretty soon, she was keeping her head shaved and shiny.

Years passed, and landlords and lovers came and went. A drunk-driving episode put Turtle in juvenile detention for 30 days. Robyn worked her way up in the restaurant business. Sometimes, Robyn crashed with Turtle in the run-down Sheppard Street townhouse that belonged to Michael Hicks, an old boyfriend of Turtle's mom who was as much of a step-dad as Turtle ever had.

Michael generally gave Turtle and her friends the run of the place. In summer, they kept the door unlocked for im-

promptu pool tournaments. There were the inevitable pair-
ings in the dark and always the throaty songs of Melissa
Etheridge, Turtle's own personal rock goddess.

Being smack in the middle of Carytown had its advantages. Babe's, for instance, Richmond's one lesbian bar, a
cozy corner pub with dull orange lights and farm tools on
the ceiling—where being too young to drink was only a
problem if you tried staying after nine. And Cary Street, the
row of restaurants and gift shops that ran by Babe's and was
always attracting a fresh crop of wide-eyed teenagers. (Richmond's *Style Weekly* called it "premium street-watching,"
for whatever an over-25 opinion was worth.)

When the Sheppard Street door was bolted and the music
was off, that usually meant something was going on between
Turtle and Michael. It was an affectionate but stormy relationship. Turtle made long escapes to her mother's South
Side trailer when they fought. Or when Turtle was trying to
spend more time with her daughter, a curly-haired little girl
named Marisa whom she had birthed at the fragile age of
13.

Marisa turned four in March of 1996, the same spring
that Turtle, now 17, and Robyn, 20, nearly drowned in the
fast-moving James. Turtle was trying to teach Robyn to
swim at 3 in the morning. They were dashed against some
rocks and knocked breathless by the cold before finding land
again, a muscly pair of tattooed ladies shivering in boxer
shorts. An impromptu duet of the Indigo Girls' "Romeo and
Juliet" clinched it as a brother-love moment; the song
bounced back at them from the railbridge above and they
raced back to the car.

It was just a few blocks down from Michael's to the three-
bedroom house on South Belmont Avenue where Turtle
moved that summer with Robyn and her on-again, off-again
girlfriend, Monique Olliver, a lanky Pittsburgh native, just
back from Navy boot camp with her long brown hair and
bangs intact. Signing the new lease was part of a fresh start
on their relationship.

Turtle joined them after a few weeks and busily began applying black paint to the walls of the bedroom at the back of the house, upstairs next to the bathroom. The last tenants had left behind a bumpy couch, and the girls carried it up to the "little room," which shared the front of the house with Robyn and Monique's bright white bedroom.

The ground floor, by contrast with the second, was wide open and public. The living room and dining room went front to back with just a rectangular archway between them. A waist-high counter defined the kitchen, which was off to the left and opened onto a grassy square of yard by means of a deck.

In time, second-hand furniture supplemented Monique's own collection and made it homey. There were rugs on the floors and a big, round table in the dining room with chairs—pushed aside sometimes for Greco-Roman wrestling matches.

The couch at the lone front window in the living room faced a television set; you parked your 7-Eleven cup or your can of Miller Genuine Draft on the coffee table at your knees and tapped your cigarette in a giant, standing ashtray. Jim Morrison of The Doors stared down sweetly from a poster on the wall to your right.

The original three were rarely the only ones home at 210 South Belmont Avenue. The little room rotated a Jax, a Melissa, and a pet python named Sheba. Also, an ever-lengthening parade of visitors began taking turns on the couch downstairs.

They came as dates; they came from Cary Street, which crossed South Belmont a block and a half away; and they came from weekly meetings of ROSMY, the Richmond Organization for Sexual Minority Youth, a support group for gay kids, where Turtle had held sway for years as everybody's model teen.

The life of Turtle Tibbs wasn't always exemplary, and she was guilty of embellishing not just her age but her adventures too. Even so, the mix of her hard start and her boundless cheer made her an inspiration: One pimply boy would follow her home to avoid a bad family situation and another for help negotiating a crush. ROSMY girls more likely longed to bed Turtle—or to *be* her. She pierced her lip; they pierced their lips. She played Melissa Etheridge on her guitar; they cultivated raspy voices and learned all the words.

The neighborhood tolerated the round-the-clock activity better than most: Late-night noise wasn't a big problem. A squad car might pull up as a Saturday night mob overflowed into the street. But the woman who lived in the house on the left only came over to bum cigarettes. And the one on the right—Robyn called her "the church lady"—seemed to be around and talkative only during the day.

She was quite fervent, though, about "those girls":

"They're a coven. They're evil," she'd tell Robyn over her yardwork or between brief sermons mentioning Jesus. "You need to get them outta your house."

Robyn would humor her, accept strange little gifts, and be on her way. But the truth was that Robyn was getting annoyed: There was never any peace, and by the time she and Monique had broken up in March of 1997 and Monique had found another place to live, the dirty work piling up inside number 210 was falling more and more to Robyn. Just this side of chaos, she would always intervene. For better or worse, she was "Dad."

"Why do I always have to do the dishes?" Robyn would shout from the sink. "I don't even eat here!"

Or, "Can somebody please take out the trash because it's full, not because I asked you to?"

Many nights, all that Robyn asked was that somebody who was 21 (or faking it with convincing ID) remember to stock beer before the stores shut down at midnight. And still, leaving the stove at the Ruby Tuesday restaurant sometime after two, she would fall into bed dry-mouthed and sleepless.

"Dad" was the only wage-earner for weeks at a time. Turtle skipped from burger-turning at McDonald's to ashtray-emptying at Babe's and eventually to a job cutting grass and whacking weeds for a gardening company called Southern Ground, with long spaces of joblessness in between.

"I guess I took on a lot by letting Turtle move in there," Robyn would say later. "More than I was expecting. When she moved in, my plans were for her to become responsible in a decent amount of time."

Instead, the red row house with the fringed rainbow flag overhanging its tiny white porch only got more crowded: It was like a beacon in the night for young, gay Richmond. You never knew who would trip up those five concrete steps.

If it wasn't pretty Sarah Franklin visiting from college or some other ex of Turtle's dragging along what Robyn considered a whole lot of unnecessary drama, it was strangers with the sole intention of hanging out—leaving their clothes on the furniture and their black boots and skateboard shoes by the front door. Or reclining under the living room window, flipping between MTV and HBO (Michael Hicks paid the cable bill).

"I don't fuckin' know what to do," Turtle told Robyn, pretending out of respect for her truest friend, her butch brother, that she was ready for it to stop. "I know lotsa people and they all love me."

In the spring and early summer of 1997, when Turtle was 18, her immediate gang included three townies around her age: Stephanie Cull, a demure pothead with wire-rimmed glasses and a pale buzzcut, who drove a gray Ford Tempo with a "Handicapped" sticker because of her juvenile rheumatoid arthritis; Domica Winckler, a tiny, unsmiling black girl who lived just around the corner in a blur of extended family; and Tracy Bitner, six-foot-one with long, bleached-blond hair, who had developed a passionate—some would say hotheaded—relationship with Turtle that winter.

Stephanie, who Turtle knew from ROSMY meetings, spent a lot of time at 210 South Belmont. You had to wonder when she ever saw the inside of the trailer that she

shared with her mother and grandmother down in Chester—
not to mention her estranged live-in girlfriend, Claire Watson, who disapproved of the South Belmont scene and
mostly stayed away.

"I came home, Stephanie was there," Robyn would remember. "I left for work, Stephanie was sleeping on the
couch. I was just like, 'You've gotta go home.' "

When Stephanie wasn't on the couch, she was in her car,
ferrying somebody to work, stopping by an ATM to dip into
her $10,000 settlement from a car accident, or just driving,
a 20-ounce Mountain Dew likely at her side. When she got
depressed, which was a good deal of the time, she would
pop Tracy Chapman's "Fast Car" into the tape deck and
cruise at top speed. Except for Tracy Chapman, Stephanie
was a rocker: Her vanity plates read "NIN" for Nine Inch
Nails. Her glove compartment was full of Pink Floyd and
Grateful Dead tapes. A window sticker that looked like a
McDonald's arch but said "Marijuana, over one billion
stoned" betrayed her other obsession. (It was also a trusty
arthritis painkiller.)

Domica, also known as "Mica," arrived at 210 South
Belmont one day with Derek, a short-term roommate who
was the household meeter-greeter at that time. "Hey, come
on and hang out at our house," he told her. Pretty soon she
was ducking in for hours at a time, sometimes just to get
away from her baby-sister responsibilities. Domica—the
only straight one in this group—was a tough-talking girl
who wore a heavy load of silver loops in her ears. The single
ring in her left eyebrow overhung the longest, curviest pair
of eyelashes.

Domica knew where to get good pot; she and Stephanie
got familiar driving over to Virginia Union University to
pick it up. Knowing Domica also hooked the South Belmont
girls into the Parkwood Avenue street scene, a mostly young
crowd of black neighbors who hovered at the corner or
shouted at each other from their porches.

2:

Stephanie was the one who brought Tracy around. They had met that winter, banished one night with their cigarettes to the back door of a friend's place in Chesterfield County. Right away, Stephanie was talking up this wild Carytown house full of gay people. Tracy was intrigued—even before she laid eyes on Turtle and fell victim to a campaign of backhanded flirting.

"You're not gay," Turtle would tell her. What about that boyfriend in high school?

"Yes I am!" Tracy protested.

"Okay, prove it to me. Kiss me."

The gauntlet had been thrown. And one day, Turtle walked right into a juicy, six-foot liplock. She was still disbelieving and pushed Tracy away. But the next time Tracy tried, between video games at a noisy arcade, Turtle liked it. Tracy moved into the South Belmont house in a matter of weeks.

There was the usual alarm about their haste. "That was way too fucking quick," Stephanie would say later. But Robyn watched with more than the wariness born of experience with infatuations. She was genuinely worried about her good buddy's attachment to Tracy.

If Stephanie and Domica sometimes verged on the submissive—with Stephanie transporting Turtle around and Domica obliging other whims—Robyn didn't mind them at all. Tracy, on the other hand, was a creep. What her fans embraced as spunky and entertaining, Robyn found loud and abrasive. The first time she shook Tracy's hand, Robyn had to refrain from sharing her thoughts with Turtle: "Are you crazy? She's a psycho killer. Why are you dating her?"

Certainly Tracy was bold with her opinions—about this ridiculous butch-versus-femme thing, for instance. Tracy herself was such a mix of types: She was a hot-tempered fighter who went mushy on matters of the heart. And while there was a prettiness about her curvy lips and dimpled chin, she might have been a football player for the size of her neck and shoulders. Not to mention the fact that she towered over six feet tall.

The combination hypnotized Turtle. She listened, rapt, while Tracy talked about her baby brother and her dream of living in Hawaii, surfing all day and bartending all night. Turtle introduced her to little Marisa, who would come by with her grandma and run around among the boots and jeans in frilly dresses. And to ROSMY, where Turtle explained her determination to help other gay teens; one day she'd be an AIDS counselor. Tracy called Turtle "Honey Bunches of Oats," or "Boo."

Their liaison lasted months, a long time on the teenage calendar, and inevitably they started to share a look. Tracy wasn't into piercing, and she wasn't interested in the high-stakes tattoo race that compelled Robyn and Turtle, who would eventually achieve a total of 15 between them. Still, the girlfriends wore their hair just the same: shaved on the sides and in the back, and long enough on top to go into a ponytail for everyday use. (Then you had long hair—sort of—when you needed it for a job or parents.) And they switched clothes around between them, Turtle's great girth sometimes offsetting the 13-inch difference in height.

Not that any of this was original. Pulling back grown-out mohawks and passing around oversized shirts and low, hip-hop–style jeans was as customary for cool girls around Carytown as the pagers inevitably hooked on every belt, job or no job.

Arguing was also normal, but sometimes it got to be too much between these two. Tracy was jealous, Turtle was a smartass—and blows were exchanged. It was never clear which one of them was responsible for the fist-sized hole in the downstairs wall at 210 South Belmont.

"They were lovey-dovey but at the same time they would fight," according to Stephanie, who was learning about feisty relationships that spring from her own efforts to brush off Claire (without punches).

But then Tracy got down on her knees in Turtle's room one day that spring and asked Turtle to marry her. She pushed her fingers into the nubby hair at the back of Turtle's neck and kissed her deeply. Turtle was in heaven. Her mind raced ahead to the planning: They'd do it next year, in the back yard of the Metropolitan Community Church—the gay church. She'd wear shorts! They'd have a certificate all done up with women's symbols. Marisa would be the flower girl.

Turtle leapt downstairs with her announcement. "I'm getting married!" she shouted, beaming at a puzzled Robyn. "Do you want to be my best man?"

And then one night at the end of May, with Turtle nowhere in sight, Tracy noticed somebody sitting at the other end of a dark party, kind of cute in a preppy way, with her shiny, black hair freshly cut along the tops of her ears. Her name was Sandy Servantez, she was Mexican, practically middle-aged at 30, and Tracy was friends with her niece. Tracy made it her business to find out that Sandy had been to the Indigo Girls show downtown. First chance she got, Tracy crossed the room.

"Didya go? Didya go?"

It wasn't the smoothest line, but it worked. Tracy was a picture of innocence when she chewed at her skinny lips and trapped your gaze with dark, pupilless eyes.

"Yeah, man, I was up there," Sandy granted, wondering, Who is this big girl? I'm with adults here.

A few weeks went by and the niece got them both out to a Richmond Braves game at the Diamond. They stayed up talking till six in the morning.

Pretty soon, Tracy was moving out of the South Belmont

Avenue house and calling it a breakup. She only took
about half of her things. Turtle was expecting her back anytime.

"Trace, is Turtle really short?"

Tracy and her new older lady were nuzzling in the ticket
line outside the Flood Zone, a former tobacco warehouse in
the old, cobble-stoned part of the city, generally swarming
with frat boys and tourists. A Richmond band called Fighting Gravity—a Turtle–Tracy favorite—was about to go on-
stage and the sidewalk was bristling with anticipation and
attitude.

"Where? Where?" Tracy dropped Sandy's hand and
seemed to shrink in her clothes. Sandy had felt this chill
more than once in four weeks of stumbling on old Turtle
haunts and into old Turtle sidekicks—and for all she knew
it was pure fear.

The girl who had parted the crowd a few feet away, crin-
kly eyes fixed on some distant point and oblivious of the
new couple, was gone. But there was no doubt. It was
Turtle.

Sandy would marvel later at her mastery of the grunge
look, repulsed as only "the other woman" could be. "Out
of that whole crowd, you could pick her out, 'cause she was
really nasty," Sandy recalled. "She had a baseball hat on,
and it was backwards. She had everything pierced on her
face. She had, like, a raggedy t-shirt and shorts down to her
damn ankles."

A few minutes later, there she was, up close and chatty,
very much the Turtle that Sandy would get to know better.

"Hey."

She was short, all right.

"Whassup?" Tracy was warm but nervous.

Sandy shook Turtle's hand and had evil thoughts:

"I was really pissed that she was there. You know, Go
away, it's my girlfriend now. Stay away. But I didn't say
anything, I wasn't mean or rude. And next thing I know,
Tracy had this different attitude. She was scared to show

me any affection. I was getting really mad. See, me and Tracy were really touchy-feely kind of people. We didn't hide anything out in public, we were all over each other.''

Making matters worse, Tracy wandered to the stage to see the show up close with Turtle and some other girls. And when Tracy came back to Sandy again, she was wiping tears from her eyes.

''Tracy, what's wrong?''

Long, annoying pause. Sandy was not liking this one bit.

''Turtle,'' came the answer.

''Fuck. What the hell is going on?''

The Matchpoint apartment complex where Sandy rented a groundlevel one-bedroom suite was an oasis of adulthood for Tracy. It was a pillowed boudoir where the lovers were reunited after Sandy's night shift as a supervisor at a window factory, and a private dining room where Sandy delivered steaming plates to her big, grinning partner.

You could tell that Sandy was proud of her independence by the way she arranged things: A neat row of videotapes against her living room wall, a handpainted photograph of her grandmother above. Matchpoint itself, a gated, hillside compound with a swimming pool and tennis courts, screamed middle-class grownup, from the tasteful beige siding to the tightly trimmed shrubbery. And Sandy had bigger plans. She'd saved enough money that she was thinking about buying a place. Sure, she was 30, but she'd always been like that. It was Sandy's nature to be mature and levelheaded.

All this struck some kind of a balance for Tracy with the wilder world at South Belmont Avenue—and yet she seemed to chafe. Later she would talk about her time with Sandy like it was some sort of medicine. ''She's supposed to be the right crowd,'' Tracy would say, parroting the advice of so many people that sometimes it had been hard for Tracy to know which lifestyle she preferred, not to mention which girlfriend.

''You need to stick with Sandy,'' Tracy's cousin Stan

told her once, "and stop hanging out with those girls.
You're really fucking up, 'cause those people, they're losers.
Sandy's there to support you in whatever you want to do,
even if you want to go back to school. You've got a good
girlfriend, don't fuck it up."

The nice Mexican girl Tracy took around to see her
mother and grandmother wasn't introduced as her lover because *nobody* could pass that test. Tracy's family had kicked
her out of the house over her first girlfriend. But as a treas-
ured friend, they adored Sandy, even hoped some of her
adult behavior would rub off.

That was probably in vain. Sandy being a pillar of responsibility didn't make Tracy one. On the contrary, she
was flailing under Sandy's doting attentions. One day she
quit her job handing out game tokens at the Windy Hill
recreation park, without a lot of explanation.

Sandy was patient. "Tracy, if you don't like it, go for
something else," she told her.

Tracy tried going door-to-door in the Richmond area raising donations for an environmental group, and it rained her
first day out. She wrote Sandy a letter from the road. "I
want to go home," she whined. The second day she quit.

"I know people and places," Sandy told her. "I can
hook you up with temp agencies. I know a manager."

No thanks. Tracy didn't know what she wanted to do.
But 9–5 office work wasn't it.

Tracy's sleeping arrangements were a little odd during this
period; she pretty much lived at both places. When Sandy
went to work, she would head over to 210 South Belmont.

"I made her move out of Turtle's room and sleep in the
little room," Sandy would remember. And you have to ad-
mire her faith. "She hated it 'cause that little sofa hurt her
back."

Tracy had a Matchpoint key, and later she would describe
the apartment complex as "home." But weekday nights
were for her buddies at South Belmont.

For a while there didn't seem to be any reason to worry.

There Tracy would be, stopping in at the window factory for a visit sometime after midnight. She'd stay an hour, sometimes two. And when Sandy knocked off work at 8 or 8:30 in the morning and phoned South Belmont, Tracy would be back at Matchpoint by 9.

But then one night in the middle of July, Tracy announced that she was confused.

"I need to tell you something," she told Sandy.

"What, honey?"

"I'm starting to miss Turtle."

Sandy took this at face value and didn't seem to understand exactly which kind of "missing" she meant.

"Well, Tracy," she said, "I understand. I'm not trying to pull you away from your friends. If you want to hang out with them more, that's fine."

"Well, I *really* miss her."

"I know, I miss my girlfriend too—my ex-girlfriend."

"I don't know what to do."

"Tracy, you know, I'm not going to force you to do anything."

But it was worse than Sandy thought. Turtle was doing things for Tracy all the time, making her breakfast, buying her flowers. Tracy eventually told her that much. She had to find out about the rest—the kissing, the cooing—from another source.

"Tracy, what's up with that?" Sandy wanted to know. "Are you going to get back together?"

Toward the end of the month, Sandy began to think that the storm had passed. Tracy was writing her love letters all the time. She'd pick up a piece of paper, jot something down about longing for Sandy, can't wait to hold her again, and then give it to her when she saw her.

"I talked to Turtle," she told Sandy. "I've got everything straightened out."

3:

On its way down from the Blue Ridge Mountains, the James River also passes through the city of Lynchburg, 110 miles west of Richmond. Lynchburg has an illustrious history too: Thomas Jefferson had a house there, and the Appomattox battlefield where the Civil War ended is close by. Tobacco and then high-technology have helped it stay on the map since. But Lynchburg is probably best known nowadays as the City of Churches and, since 1971, home of Jerry Falwell's Liberty University.

Conservative Christians are Lynchburg's most audible citizens, down to the Christian rock on the radio, and the atmosphere is not always easy for lesbians and gay men. There's neither a gay bar in town nor enough gay political clout to call attention to the undercurrent of hostility. Still, plenty of gay people live there contentedly—as teenagers, even.

In June 1997, a friend of Turtle's from ROSMY named Dana Vaughan moved out to Lynchburg to try and salvage a long-distance romance. Dana, a round, pink-faced blonde with clear plastic glasses, was not so sure about the romance after a week in town. But it was clear that she was going to need a job.

Dana, whom Turtle had dubbed "Joe," went looking for work on July 2nd at a Lynchburg Taco Bell and noticed a slim girl with short, dark brown hair packing burritos into paper bags behind the counter. She spoke with a hint of Lynchburg's sharp drawl and her name was Stacey Hanna. Two days later, on the 4th, they were friends enough to get up early and drive to Richmond. It was planned as a day trip—"I was supposed to be back at 4 in Lynchburg," Dana would recall.

Richmond beckoned wildly to both of them. Dana was homesick and now fully over her Lynchburg girlfriend. Stacey, recently 18 and eager to exercise her adulthood, was up for *anything* to take her away from the city of her unhappy youth, even for a day. Dana would show her around Richmond, introduce her to some people. And man, did Dana know some cool lesbians.

When the pair stopped in at 210 South Belmont Avenue, it was everything that Lynchburg was not. Turtle was up and grinning at the sight of Dana climbing the front steps.

"Oh my God! Joe!" Turtle shrieked.

"Yo, Turtle!"

They stomped around for a minute, two wide backs clenched in a bear hug.

"I can't let you leave. You gotta stay!" Turtle teased, throwing a glance at the cute new girl in the doorway, who now revealed a shiny set of braces. At five-four, Stacey was taller than the other two and far more delicate in a boyish way; she pushed a wave of hair across her temple. And when Turtle heard her speak in a voice that was high and sweet, but rough around the edges, she was sold.

"I asked Stacey if she wanted to stay too," remembers Dana. They even took a walk around the block to talk about it. "And, I mean, all she had to do was say *No*."

If Robyn wasn't thrilled about the extra roommate, the extra rent check shut her up fast. Stacey and Dana got kitchen cleanup work right away at the Chesapeake Bagel Bakery, a sandwich shop at the other end of the Willow Lawn shopping center from Robyn's Ruby Tuesday job.

Stacey also won Robyn over with gifts, and left her frisky but obedient notes around the house, like "Hi, Dad. Love, Stacey."

Monique and Dana got presents too. But it was Turtle's approval that Stacey craved most—and shopped for. She gave her an expensive Tommy Hilfiger jersey and a round-faced green watch with a brown leather band. And then, in case there was any doubt about the tenor of Stacey's affections, one day Turtle followed a trail of 12 romantic greeting cards through the house. Another time, Stacey said it with kitchen condiments.

Oh c'mon, the roommates were starting to think.

"Mustard, whipped cream, ketchup all out in the street with her name in it is a little bit much," Dana would suggest. " 'I love you, Turtle' or 'I heart you' or I don't know what the heck it was. Then she got mad at me 'cause I came home and drove over it."

At first, Turtle liked all this; she liked Stacey—her directness, the way she walked, even her prim refusal to drink or curse. Turtle obliged her repeated requests for a verse or two of the Indigo Girls' "Romeo and Juliet" and shared in Stacey's excitement about coming out to her Aunt Lisa one day at the Bagel Bakery. The aunt was fine about it—and not surprised. Turtle knew how hard it had been for Stacey to approach her mother about being gay.

"She felt like nobody would understand and everybody would look down on her because she was going through all this," Turtle would remember later. She, by contrast, was a friend Stacey could confide in. "She could trust me," Turtle would say.

The question of their intimacy was confusing, though, even to their closest friends. They kissed a little and were cozy enough that people figured they were sleeping together—not just sharing Turtle's queen-size bed as roommates, sometimes with Dana as well and sometimes without.

That was definitely the impression for Kevin Day, the guy back in Lynchburg who had always had a thing for Stacey. He met Turtle in the middle of July when she drove out there with Stacey and Dana to pick up some of their belongings.

"So is this your new girl?" he inquired that day, walking the two blocks to Waffle House from the hillside apartment on Memorial Avenue where Stacey had lived with her friends Michelle and Mike before moving to Richmond. Stacey didn't answer him.

Kevin was angry with her for moving away. But he drove the visitors around in the back of his white truck, and they picked up some clothes, cd's, a pet rabbit—and got back on the road. Whether or not Kevin had ever been Stacey's boyfriend (*No way*, she told her new friends), she was definitely done with this guy.

Sort of like Turtle was done with Stacey.

The truth was that Turtle didn't see her flirtation with Stacey turning into a love affair. If Stacey did, well that was too bad. She'd get over it.

Instead, Turtle was beginning to realize that it was Tracy she wanted. At times she was torn—Stacey, Tracy; even their names confused her—but at the end of the day there was no question at all about which girl was number one.

This important change of heart from the Queen Bee of South Belmont Avenue coincided with some other rude awakenings. Stacey's roommates discovered that many of their nice new wallets, t-shirts, and hats had been shoplifted. Dana was the one to pick up on it first: "I left her in the mall and she came back with a handful of stuff," she would recall.

More important, though, was learning that this new girl was interfering in their already complicated teenage love lives, inventing drama where there was none, switching stories around to her own liking. At first, it seemed, for sport. But no, Stacey was not having fun.

On the contrary, Stacey was tortured by Turtle's expiring interest—and most of all, by the undeniable signs that Turtle and Tracy were rekindling. There Stacey would be, walking out of the kitchen one day, humming along to Melissa Etheridge and looking pretty good in nothing but a sports bra and big, baggy overalls. And there they would be, lips together, on the couch.

Stacey didn't exactly *reason* that transparent little lies would keep the couple apart and propel Turtle into her own arms. But out they came. "Turtle said she was going to propose to me tonight," she told Tracy. "Tracy loves Sandy, not you," she told Turtle. And so on.

Most of the time, her motives were so obvious as to be pitiful. Dana and Stephanie sometimes made fun, while Domica took the position that the whole thing was ridiculous.

None of this, however, stopped Stacey from inventing ever-more-creative scenarios. Once, knowing that Tracy was within earshot downstairs, Stacey made it sound like she was getting in the shower with Turtle. Another time, she told Tracy over the phone, "Turtle left with some girl. And she was talking all kinds o' nasty stuff to her on the phone. So I think she's goin' out on a date."

This definitely worked to make Tracy crazy; she was obsessively on the alert. When Stacey wrote "I love you, Turtle" in the middle of the street with toilet paper—this time protected by a string of orange traffic cones—Tracy went outside, got in her car, ran it over, and then ran it over again.

Except for the kick of watching Tracy twist, Stacey's little tricks and bold displays of affection didn't always work to her own advantage. If Tracy found out that Stacey and Turtle had plans, then she would get down there before they had a chance to walk out the door—sometimes even when it meant standing up poor Sandy back at Matchpoint.

"C'mon, Boo," Tracy would tell Turtle, as if overcome by spontaneity and unaware of the conflict. "Let's go do something."

It was a test. And it worked. Five minutes later, Turtle was climbing in the passenger side of Tracy's big white car with a casual "Later, Stacey!"

It wasn't always enough, though, to leave Stacey in the dust, humiliated but somehow unrepentant. At times, they made it clear that they would put an end to her behavior with physical force if it came to that.

"Don't fucking touch my girlfriend or I'll beat your ass!" Tracy shouted once, stiffening to her full height for a slow, menacing walk in Stacey's direction. "Leave us alone!" Turtle growled.

PART TWO

A Fatal Lie

"This whole incident made me feel really dumb, 'cause there's a lot of clues I could have put together. When they say it over and over again in the trial, it makes so much sense. And then I'm like, 'Man, I wonder why I didn't figure that out.'"

—Robyn

4:

Summer in Richmond, to paraphrase psychedelic Southern author Tom Robbins, is like the inside of a watermelon that's been hollowed out by napalm. Not only can't you breathe, but the remnants of something sweet are enough to drive you crazy. Some days the nearest breeze is a full two hours east at the beach.

Phish, the indie rock band of the moment, played an open-air, sold-out concert at the Virginia Beach Amphitheater on the second-to-last Monday in July, and Turtle brought her crew—minus Domica and Tracy. She was enjoying her favorite toy: double sticks, a Native American–inspired game that involves bouncing a piece of wood between a pair of sticks, when a spacey young man approached her.

"Can I play with 'em?" he inquired.

"Yeah. Sure." Turtle handed them over and he set the sticks bobbing at his own, slower pace.

"Y'all looking for anything?" he asked distractedly.

"Looking for what?"

"Acid." For example.

"Sure!" Turtle was up for that. And so were the others—a small crowd including Stacey, Stephanie, and Dana, shouting at each other now over the music.

"I'll give you two free ones for letting me use your double sticks," the guy told Turtle. "But you gotta pay for the rest."

Lucky day: This would jibe nicely with their plans. Stephanie's mom was on a business trip and her grandmother was vacationing in Atlanta. Claire was gone too, having been sent packing once and for all in recent weeks. The trailer would be empty for days.

The girls forked over some cash and put the little slips of paper on their tongues right away. The music melted into a soft ripple, and then Stephanie—as skilled as anyone at driving high—floated them away to Green Leigh.

They would stay on and off for three days, the hours flying by in a pleasant mist of sisterly affection and sleeplessness. Outside, it rained a lot; inside, the living room became lined with mattresses, decorated here and there with small piles of dirty dishes and makeshift ashtrays. Every now and then, the floor would stop moving and they would take another hit of acid.

The girls with responsibilities left and came back; Stacey trained for a new waitressing job on the Annabel Lee riverboat. Domica joined the group at one point—and didn't like the drugs much. But she may have been the exception.

"We had found our happy place in life and that was it," Turtle would remember. "There was us and the trailer, there was nobody else anywhere. We never thought it was gonna end. We were going to be here for the rest of our lives. And we were in a movie. That's my thing: Life is just a movie, and you have to play a part."

Stacey herself seemed to be having fun. On the surface, at least, she was laid-back and pleasant, blithely deflecting come-ons from one tripping friend and cuddling with Turtle when she was given the chance.

But a patchwork of events that week suggests that she was beginning to think seriously about the hostility coming her way from the couple she had been trying so hard to destroy. Acid can make a person paranoid, but it also tends to sharpen perceptions and bring even the loftiest delusions to their knees.

There were casual mentions of a trip to Lynchburg maybe sometime soon. But Stacey would also cry out more directly for help, look outside this tight circle, and admit she was afraid.

It's just that she wasn't moving in a straight line toward

a solution. She could too easily be swayed back into complacency, even out-and-out joy, by the pockets of sweetness that Turtle was capable of. It was a combination—sweetness and terror—that Stacey was used to.

"Debbie, it's Stacey. I need you to come get me."

"Stacey, what?" Debbie Parker was caught off guard. It was Tuesday at about 2 in the afternoon. She was behind her desk, just outside Lynchburg at the Bedford County Department of Social Services, in the same courthouse basement where Stacey had reached her in various states of panic a hundred times before. But right then she had somebody in her office.

"I need you to come and get me," Stacey repeated. Debbie wondered where exactly she was and why she would need a ride. Brawling with her mom? In trouble with that horrible boyfriend of hers? Maybe she was still in Richmond. Debbie just didn't have the time to find out.

"Stacey, I need a number where I can call you back. I need to call you back. I've got some people with me."

"I can't give you a number. I'll call *you* back."

Debbie Parker had known Stacey Hanna for almost five years at that point, probably as well as anyone else. A tall, frenetic, pixie-haired mother of four, a shoulder to cry on for children all over Bedford County, Debbie had started counseling Stacey when she tried to kill herself in 1992. Three years later, as Stacey told Debbie, the girl endured the one-two punch of her life: She told her mother that her father had been molesting her for years—and her mother's response was, That's not your father. A second suicide attempt followed.

Stacey had since nurtured big hopes of prosecuting this man, long ago divorced from Stacey's mother. And it was Debbie's job to "get her ready" to testify in an open court if and when that time ever came.

Once, she got close but backed down, feeding Debbie's fear that Stacey didn't have the support at home that she would need for a sexual abuse investigation. As Debbie saw it, Stacey's relationship with her mother was simply too troubled on its own.

Something about Stacey's pending adulthood—she would be 18 on March 29, 1997—had convinced her to try again, and Lieutenant Ricky Garner at the Bedford County Sheriff's Department had reopened the case in October 1996.

Debbie had seen Stacey several times since. During their last visit, in June, Stacey fidgeted but seemed okay. She was talking about going into the service, mentioned something about going down to Richmond to see a recruiter. Debbie had suggested that she go back and finish high school first.

Perhaps it was hope that kept Debbie's overworked brain from flashing Code Red that Tuesday afternoon in July. Later, the regret would consume her.

"When she did not call back, I cannot honestly say now that I even thought about it later.

"Of course, had she said, 'I'm in serious trouble,' I would have said, 'Okay, hang on just one second, Stace, let me put you on hold.' And I would have said to these people, 'I'm sorry, I need to step outside and make a call.'"

After two days of missing Tracy in the trailer—well, Turtle missed her—they piled back into Stephanie's car and headed up to the city to fetch her. That night, Tracy took her first-ever hit of acid and the trailer party continued as before.

There were some brave excursions outside their small rectangular world on this second lap: The group ambled over to visit their friend Mike and played with his baby. And at one point, everybody left Turtle and Tracy alone in the trailer for a couple of hours while they listened to music—and fought about Tracy's hankering for a radical new hairdo.

"I wanna shave my head," Tracy said. Again and again all week. Everybody but Turtle and Dana loved the idea.

"Don't you shave your head," Turtle snarled. "You'll

look like a fuckin' dude. I'm not gonna be with a dude. Plain and simple. You'll look all butch."

And then there was a confusing picture of calm that suggested the tug of war over Turtle might finally be in the past, that Tracy and Stacey might just coexist in her life without any more trouble. Not that a drug binge is a good time to draw conclusions.

The third and last night of the acid trip, Claire showed up at the trailer in the dark in hopes of telling Stephanie that she had gotten her hands on some tickets to the Lilith music festival. She also wanted to make sure Stephanie wasn't hurting herself with those drugs. Bruised as Claire was by her difficulties with Stephanie, this very trailer and Stephanie's own bed had been her home until recently; she felt entitled to make occasional stabs at normalizing their relationship.

It was Turtle who came to the door, warning darkly against going inside.

"You shouldn't go in there," she said. "They don't need you. You'll just scare Stephanie. You know, they're flipping out."

Likely, this was Turtle's tricky little way of keeping Claire from dragging down the party. But Claire didn't want to risk a scene and so she left.

Trying again the next day, she stumbled on a rare moment of sobriety. There were signs that someone had started to clean up. Why didn't you come in last night? they wanted to know. They had needed her there—for a change. Had wanted somebody with a clear head to help them through a bad patch with the acid.

At the time, Claire was furious with Turtle for having manipulated the situation to keep her away. And then at Stephanie, who accused her, in so many words, of snooping.

"I didn't like her hanging out with them," Claire would say, trying to explain the mutual paranoia. "I had my own jealousies 'cause I didn't spend as much time with her. But it was more I was concerned for her. And she didn't see it that way."

Later, though, Claire was haunted instead by the very first sight she had seen as the trailer door slammed shut behind her on the way inside: Turtle, stretched out on one of the mattresses, was quite comfortably sandwiched between her two women. She had one arm around Tracy's shoulders, and Stacey had completely enveloped Turtle's other side.

"It was so symbolic," Claire says. "It was totally what was going on. I think Stacey may have known what Turtle was doing with her arm around Tracy. But she totally ignored it. She tried harder and harder to get Turtle's attention.

"For Tracy and Turtle it was kinda like a joke. It was like, 'Oh man, this girl doesn't even know that we really wanna be together. And she won't get the hint.'

"Turtle was totally leading her on," Claire adds. "How was she supposed to know?"

It was Stacey herself who finally dragged an electric shaver through Tracy's long, wavy hair that Thursday night. She did it upstairs at the South Belmont house, with an enthusiastic and noisy audience. Turtle pouted downstairs with her guitar. And then the cheering stopped and there was Tracy at her side, in a baseball cap.

"Turtle, don't be mad at me," she cooed, inching her bristly dome out into the light.

It appears to have been happenstance that Stacey was the one standing over Tracy's head, removing all the blond that Turtle liked so much. But the haircut precipitated Stacey's second plea for help by mere hours, and so you have to wonder what was said—or left unsaid.

The South Belmont crowd went to the weekly ROSMY meeting that night, minus Dana. And afterwards, Stacey spoke with a couple of boys drinking coffee. They were seated at the end of a long table at the back of Bidder's Suite, a dark, smoky Alice in Wonderland-theme coffee shop-and-art gallery in a basement under West Grace Street. It was a first date of sorts for Peter and Will.

"I'm scared," Stacey told them. "Turtle and them are

mad at me. And you know, I think they might get violent if I don't do something.''

"What's going on? Why are they mad?" Will asked her. He was confused. He knew Turtle, at least, to be a toughie, but nice.

"Oh just because. I'm not really sure—they just don't like me.''

Will would remember this conversation as frustrating and vague. ''I was trying to see if there was anywhere else for her to go. And she was talking about how there wasn't. There was nowhere else for her to go.''

Maybe Stacey wasn't really ready to leave. Noticing the approaching storm was a big step, but the will to move out of its way required something else. She was beginning to learn—from Debbie Parker, perhaps—that bringing voice to her private terrors might actually get her somewhere one day, but it was still no more than an idea.

Meanwhile, she seemed almost inured to the terror, possibly even attached to it. Even as Stacey was considering and rejecting escape that Thursday night, she was busy crafting another tall tale that would make her roommates madder. With an eye, presumably, toward getting Turtle jealous.

Oddly, she picked Dana's current love interest—a girl named Sharon—for this next spectacle. Stacey had chatted a lot with Sharon at the ROSMY meetings and then, to her roommates back home, cast this casual friendliness as a passionate attraction of Sharon's.

"I don't want you to be mad at me, but there's something I've got to tell you," Stacey told Dana, who had stayed home from the meeting with a cold. "Sharon told me that she liked me and not you. And that, you know, she really wants to start dating and all that.''

"Aw shit," was all Dana could say. What a slap in the face!

But then Dana got to thinking.

"I thought I knew Sharon," Dana would say later. "And she's not the person to just come out and say, 'I like you.' That seemed a little weird. And so I talked to Turtle.''

"No way. That's not what happened at all," Turtle told her—fuming. Turtle had been right there at the ROSMY meeting; Turtle had seen it all. "Stacey was all over *Sharon*."

Clearly, Stacey's obsession with Turtle had superseded all other concerns. Dana, her main buddy in this crowd, was only a pawn now, in the service of positioning Stacey where she was not: the center of attention, the object of Turtle's desire.

As for Turtle, she didn't care about the Sharon story either. What she cared about was Stacey's audacity. By now she was genuinely riled by her meddling—as well as by the brutal fact that, as the days went by, Stacey's stories about Tracy were starting to look a little bit true.

It was just sinking in: Tracy wasn't doing anything at all to sever her ties with Sandy.

5:

President Lincoln went to Richmond just before the end of the Civil War in 1865 to see for himself that the Confederate Capital was defeated and burning. He arrived by boat unannounced, stepped out of the James River at a place called Rocketts Landing, and walked right up through the smoky streets.

In the summer of 1997, the Landing was still a wide open patch of earth, a rare break in the modern riverfront between cargo docks, train bridges, and paved traffic ramps. It was not by oversight, though, or some homage to open space that the lot had endured: In modern times, Rocketts Landing was for parking. A steady stream of tourists left their cars behind there to board a replica of an old-time paddlewheel riverboat called the Annabel Lee.

Off hours, the Annabel Lee bobbed gracefully at a knot of trees. Out on the water, it was a non-stop, climate-controlled party, with bingo and singing waitresses at lunch, ballroom dancing after dinner, and stopovers on Tuesdays at the old Westover, Evelynton, and Berkeley plantations downriver. The onboard galley was endlessly sending out crab cakes, sugar-cured ham, and slow-cooked beef.

Stacey carried lunch-hour cocktails across the deck of the Annabel Lee that last Friday in July. It was a new job, but no problem for her at all. Stacey loved a crowd, and the tourists found her mannerly and hard-working. It was a stretch working two places—especially as the Chesapeake Bagel Bakery had begun to pale by comparison with the more elegant riverboat scene—but she'd done it before.

Something was still quite wrong, though. She tried Debbie Parker again from the Annabel Lee as lunch wound down on Friday, but Debbie was busy, the secretary said, taking down the message that Stacey would call again.

Returning home after her shift, Stacey was on edge. The faces and the shops she passed along the way were getting familiar, but not with the sense of belonging that she wanted. Richmond had become like Lynchburg, her passions all mixed up with her pains. She wanted to see Turtle, she knew that, but she was also afraid.

Moving up the stairs, she was vaguely aware of guitar music. And voices. And then Turtle was right there in the hall.

"Why did you lie about Sharon?" Turtle wanted to know, having just spent the afternoon with the woman in question and gotten all wound up about it. There was no waiting for an answer, though. Stacey's "What are you talking about?" was entirely muffled by a vicious smack. And then another.

Turtle's hands seemed to fly out of nowhere, stinging Stacey's face and coming down in solid fists on the back of her head, again and again. Stacey's raised arms were a flimsy shield, even as she dropped to the floor. Turtle got a handful of hair and yanked her back to her feet.

"This is for lying!" Turtle pronounced.

"No!" Stacey shrieked. "Stop it. Stop!"

Turtle let go of her hair but continued slapping and asked, "Why did you lie?"

Answering that question was as far from Stacey's abilities right then as wrestling Turtle to the floor; in the same way that Turtle was physically stronger, it also must have felt to Stacey like she was in control of the words.

Well, maybe not all of them: Stacey scrambled to think of something hard and mean—anything to hurt her back. And of course there was just one thing. As powerless and miserable as Stacey was, Turtle's Achilles' heel was still within her reach. Once again, though, she confused her need to be noticed with her desire for peace:

"Tracy don't want you!" Stacey threw out clumsily,

breaking down now into tears, her batterer unflinching.

Stacey made a dash for the stairs at this point. But then there was Domica too, and Stacey muttered something about "bitch" and that was enough to pull Domica into this brawl. Domica's knee swung up into a kick, but her balance was off, and her foot slammed Turtle in the eye.

The stairs seemed to come up under them without warning, and they banged around between walls and steps to keep themselves upright. All three stumbled down into the living room and then Turtle paused to finger the left side of her face and to glare at Domica.

"Shit, man!" Turtle barked. "You kicked me." Her hand came away bloody from her nose.

Stacey's attackers retreated to the second floor now, and she curled up in a ball on the couch. She listened to the cars in the street, heard Turtle go back to her guitar, and wondered when she would stop crying. And who the hell she could call.

Family friend Lisa Danner—the Aunt Lisa she had come out to at the Bagel Bakery—picked up on the first ring. But it took her a moment to understand what was going on because Stacey was whispering. "They're hitting me," she hissed. "I have to go home."

Lisa got the Richmond police on the phone; they would dispatch a unit to the house right away, they told her. But instead of cops, Robyn bounced in the door, and right over to the trembling, unhappy child on the sofa.

"Hey, man, what's wrong?" she inquired. Robyn had been drinking; she was hoping for a short and lighthearted answer to this question. But Stacey just shook her head. Her face was stained with tears and her lips quivered slightly, suggesting she might cry again anytime.

Robyn's opinion for some time now was that this girl was over her head in this crowd. Her first instinct was to protect Stacey from whatever was going on in the house lately. But that was outweighed just now—and most of the time—by Robyn's ties to Turtle. It was a mix of not wanting

to butt into her best friend's business and not wanting to
play Dad every damn day of the week that steered her clear,
whenever possible, of this brewing battle. A little peace-
making couldn't hurt, though.

"I know what'll cheer ya up," Robyn promised, running
up the stairs, grabbing an equally somber Turtle, tissue to
her bloody face, and all the while mumbling something
about Romeo and Juliet. "C'mon, we gotta sing her the
song!" she told Turtle.

But there was no way. Turtle would be dragged downstairs but she would not perform.

"No," she said firmly. "If you pull out the you-have-
to-because-you're-my-best-friend, then I'll do it. But I really
don't want to."

"Please don't make her," Stacey mumbled from the
couch. Don't get Turtle mad again, for God's sake. She was
shaking her head back and forth and seemed to mean it.

Okay, Robyn was done here. "Whatever," she said. "I'm
going to have a good time someplace else. You guys are all
sad." And then she went out again through the front door.

The scene that Robyn left behind that Friday evening—the
summer sun was still high, but by now it wasn't afternoon
anymore—was much more serious a conflict than Robyn
believed, and the pressure was building. The question was:
Were the traces of love between these two likely to have a
calming effect—or heat them to a full boil?

The sight of Turtle standing over her now at the couch
had a strange, exhilarating effect on Stacey. She loved Turtle
at that moment, perhaps as much as she ever had, despite
the phone call for help and despite the warm swelling on
her face. Stacey may have felt, as people sometimes do, that
her bruises were not such a bad sign.

It could also be argued that her storytelling about Sharon
had, in fact, worked out okay. It was Turtle's attention that
she longed for, and here she had it, full on. The physical
sensation of their violent encounter was familiar, and
vaguely sexual, for both of them.

Stacey had been genuinely afraid of Turtle a minute ago, and several times that week. It wasn't that she now managed to suppress her terror, but that she wanted so badly to believe it was over. Meanwhile, she clung to the make-believe: Maybe there was some jealousy there after all, she told herself, maybe on some level Turtle couldn't bear the thought of Stacey and Sharon together.

While that's not at all what was going on in Turtle's head, she was equally confused. She was still furious, and she was not sorry for the beating. But she was charmed at Stacey's resilience—and as Stacey now muttered a vague apology, she loved her willingness to affirm Turtle's upper hand.

Stacey felt better too for the gesture, and in her rapture, invited Turtle to dinner.

"Go on, get dressed," she said, coquettishly. She was taking her out, she announced. It was going to be a surprise; she had a plan. "Just get dressed—and look decent."

Stacey disappeared now for a while with Peter, the friend she had panicked with just the night before at the Bidder's Suite. And when they came back—with a bouquet of flowers for Turtle—Turtle had put on a clean t-shirt, a nice pair of khaki slacks, a white button-down blouse, and a black leather vest. Stacey brushed her own hair out and slipped into a short green dress. The only thing on her long, bare legs was the piece of string that she always wore around her right ankle.

"Come on," she told Turtle. "We're going somewhere." Peter was giving them a ride.

Stacey's plans for the evening remained a mystery to Turtle until they had crossed the cobbled streets down near the Flood Zone, and Rocketts Landing opened up in front of them. They boarded the Annabel Lee now with two free passes that Stacey had been saving with exactly this in mind.

When the boat pulled out into the James at 7:30, they were seated for dinner, a long, slow meal next to a married couple from New York who told the girls that they had met on the boat 15 years earlier—but gotten together only after the woman chased away the guy's clingy ex. Stacey whispered to Turtle that this was *their* story too.

"Oh, y'all are so cute," the woman, big and round with an advanced pregnancy, told them.

Stacey couldn't help but agree.

"Aren't we?"

She looked at Turtle.

"Uh, yeah," came Turtle's reply.

After dinner, they visited the upper deck, where there was an open-air dance floor, and the 18-year-olds—bruises already beginning to surface on their faces—slow-danced. When it started to drizzle, Stacey said she was cold, and Turtle relinquished her long-sleeved shirt. The music kept playing, but only the most committed dancers stayed in the rain.

Turtle herself would say later that, swaying there together on the Annabel Lee, they were closer than they had ever been. "For a second I totally forgot about Tracy," she said. "And everything was all right."

Tracy was out with Sandy that night, and completely in the dark about the reason for Stacey's thrashing. "It's just some stuff Stacey said. Stuff that wasn't true," Turtle explained vaguely over the phone. But Tracy knew that they were dining out alone, and she had earlier endured some of her own bullshit from Stacey, more about Turtle "proposing."

One thing, perhaps, was ever clearer in Tracy's thoughts: Her life would be a lot easier if Stacey—and Sandy, as a matter of fact—would just go away and leave her and Turtle alone.

And here was a solution: Stacey was talking about going back to Lynchburg but didn't have a ride? Okay: Tracy passed on the word that she would drive her home the following Wednesday night, if she didn't find anything sooner. If this beating hadn't already sent her off somewhere on her own.

6:

The wet heat limits your options on a Richmond summer Saturday. You can rent a rubber raft and run the rapids on the James. You can stand over a barbecue grill and press a beer to your forehead. Or you can shuttle quickly between air conditioners.

Dana and Stacey could have done worse that last Saturday afternoon than Willow Lawn shopping center, which housed not just Chesapeake Bagel Bakery and Ruby Tuesday, opening directly onto sweaty outdoor parking lots, but also a fully refrigerated mall. Both girls were off today, but Robyn needed a ride to work and Dana had a car. On the turn into Willow Lawn, Robyn pressed a five dollar bill into Stacey's hand.

"You have to promise. Somebody's gotta have some beer there when I get back at 2. Okay?"

"Yeah, okay."

Pretty soon Stacey and Dana were enjoying bagels from the customer side of the counter at Chesapeake, staring out at the parked cars, wondering if they were going to talk about Sharon. Or Turtle. Or Stacey's swollen face. Nah.

It was just a few steps to the Dollar Tree, a kitschy fluorescent wonderland of Water Shooters, sunglasses, dog chews, and plastic toys. Wandering was the point here, more than buying. But down at the end of aisle four, Stacey hovered at the twist-tie dispensers.

And then, oh shit, she had something in her clothes. Dana hated it when she did that. What if they got caught? A crimson wave climbed Dana's neck and burned her ears. They both left the store.

"Hey look, they're hugga-hugga orange," Stacey beamed when the coast was clear. She presented a package of three utility knives—boxcutters—in bright plastic sheaths. Hugga-hugga orange was Turtle's favorite color.

Cathy Wilson, Stacey's tense and by-now perplexed mother, called the South Belmont house a little before 3:30 that afternoon. Distracted as she was by an impending move to Florida, not to mention the summertime demands of her two young sons, her focus was on getting Stacey back to Lynchburg.

"Tracy's driving me home on Wednesday," Stacey assured her. "It'll be late. Like eleven."

And then she joined her friends at the small black lacquered table in the dining room that had replaced the big round one when Monique left. There was also a pullout sofabed against the right wall since Monique's departure, and some of them sat there.

The tools of home tattooing were laid out before them, such as they were: several bottles of ink—red, purple, green, and blue—a roll of paper towels, and Stacey's stolen merchandise from earlier, already torn triumphantly from their plastic sack.

The steel blades arrived entirely sheathed in the orange handles. You pushed at a small black lever with your thumb and slid it, clicking, along a series of notches, until a sharp edge finally emerged at the top. Each blade was scored at half-inch intervals, marking out a row of steel sections that could be broken off and discarded one at a time as they dulled, always revealing a fresh edge. Sliding your thumb back down the notches, the blade was just as easily retracted into the plastic between uses.

The girls discussed design. And then they began very slowly cutting into the soft triangles of flesh between thumb and forefinger with the first curves of one tiny circle each—only three tattooers at a time because there were that many boxcutters.

Blood ran from their hands. And at times, the rush to

keep enough ink in the wound overwhelmed their efforts to be precise about the shape.

Piercing your own skin with a sharp object is less painful than allowing someone else to make the cuts. But even as each girl chose her own speed, the boxcutters stung. The girls grimaced, and some were less comfortable than others with the steady release of blood. A rash of giggling would be interrupted by a gasp and then another dab with a paper towel.

Between turns with a knife, they leaned in to follow the others' handiwork so as not to stray too far from the official motif: tiny blue turtles—"with tails," to make them look like women's symbols.

There were variations, though. While Turtle, Stacey, Stephanie, and Dana stuck with turtles, Domica turned her circle into a smiley face instead. And Turtle worked out a spiral shape on the back of Stephanie's neck.

7:

When Saturday's punishing sun finally set, Sandy and Tracy were finishing up at a backyard cookout over in the West End. They headed back to Sandy's place with the windows all the way down in her gray Nissan pickup, and then they collapsed. Sandy reached for the button on her phone machine and was not expecting Turtle's spunky voice.

"Hey, we're going to Baby Shane's party. Why don'tcha come over?"

There was a pause and then, "Bring Sandy too!"

Turtle had called for Tracy before but "Bring Sandy too"? And who or what was Baby Shane?

Gimme a break, thought Sandy. She was queasy at the idea of sharing Tracy, and went to the kitchen for a beer. No way, she thought, longing suddenly for the old wait-in-the-car days. I know how Tracy's gonna be. Tracy's gonna ignore me. Then she caught her lover's puppy-dog stare over the top of her beer can and succumbed.

"Tracy, you wanna go? We can go."

The South Belmont house was jumping. The bass line of a rap song vibrated out onto the sidewalk. Domica and Turtle were dancing in the living room when Tracy and Sandy appeared, and then there was a group leap to the door— thumbs first. *Look what we got today!* Little blue tattoos. *They're turtles, dude!* Cool.

Even Stacey had one—Stacey?

"You still here?" Tracy asked her, dropping onto the couch next to Stephanie and Dana. "Didn't they kick your ass last night?"

"Yeah . . ." Stacey was smiling and shy, but trying to appear confident. Her face was just swollen enough to skew her features slightly.

"It's cool, man," said Turtle.

"It's all better now, we're all over it," echoed Stacey.

So what about Turtle's black eye? God forbid somebody thinks Stacey whupped her.

"Yeah, man, I fuckin' knocked her down. And Mica was gonna kick her and got me in my fuckin' eye."

As if to mark their peace with ceremony, Turtle and Stacey traded some face jewelry.

"Let me have that ring right there." Turtle pointed to Stacey's eyebrow.

"All right."

A quick twist of Stacey's wrist and there it was. Turtle threaded it through her lip.

Sandy was amazed, maybe repulsed. But she was curious, and couldn't help but notice that Turtle was curious about her too. It was as if this was the best that either of them could do with the hostility bristling between them; giving in to a confrontation wasn't worth the risk of losing Tracy to the other side.

"Where else are you pierced, Turtle?" Sandy inquired politely, and the answer was less interesting than she had expected: Turtle simply stuck out her tongue.

Later, Sandy took Tracy out to her truck for a lecture about "affection." And a plea. Maybe Tracy would come share her bed and leave the kiddies? It wasn't that Sandy was shocked or scared, or so she would say later, but rather bored—and jealous.

"'I really don't like being here," Sandy told Tracy. "You're ignoring me again."

"Oh c'mon, let's stay. Let's stay a little while," Tracy cooed, punctuating her counter-plea with a soft kiss.

But now the pickup was filling up behind them. Stacey, Turtle, Domica, Stephanie, Dana, and another girl who was also openly smitten with Turtle tonight were quietly taking seats in the open-air bed. And then not so quietly as the lovebirds lingered.

Hey, let's go to Baby Shane's party!

Let's go!

It was a short drive to the Boulevard, the broad avenue that separates Carytown from the Fan, and then a few blocks up away from the river. They parked outside a small house with a high fence in back and walked a frisky bedroom gauntlet of drunken gay boys that left them at the back door.

Descending to the yard, Sandy learned from Turtle that Baby Shane was the junior member of Richmond's Shane "family" of drag queens. The group settled into a face-to-face pair of benches and discussed the shortage of beer. Tracy and Sandy shared a lone Budweiser, and finally their host appeared.

There were hugs all around and then a murmur of disapproval from young Shane about the seating arrangement— Tracy up close and snuggly with Sandy instead of his good friend Turtle. He rolled his eyes, bemused more than interested, and strutted back inside.

Stacey, on the other hand, couldn't be happier about the public viewing of the couple. This was no figment of her own imagination, no abstract obsession for Turtle to brush off: Tracy and Sandy were "together." And when Sandy wandered indoors to find the bathroom and Tracy followed to speak to a friend, Stacey was right there at Turtle's ear.

"You know, I wouldn't go inside if I were you," she warned, darkly.

"Why? What do you mean?"

"Tracy and Sandy are having sex."

"Right."

It was a lame gesture but just the moment to make it. Turtle's hackles were up. And Stacey kept on, as desperately as always, but now relishing Turtle's attention.

"She doesn't want you anymore," she said. "She wants Sandy."

* * *

Half of the group crossed Carytown by foot sometime before midnight. The others picked up an 18-pack of Icehouse
in the truck and somebody got ahold of a bottle of Night
Train wine. Domica went around the corner for a while to
talk to some friends, and everybody else went to South Belmont, where Turtle and Sandy resumed their mutual examination.

"Hey, I hear you have a guitar," Turtle told Sandy.
"You wanna see mine?"

Turtle's room always looked as if a strong wind had just
knocked through. And with two extra 18-year-olds camping
there lately, it was a hurricane path of clothing, dishes, and
cd cases. There was a loveseat in the back corner, across
from a stereo stand where Monique's TV had once been.
Mostly, people sat on the big bed.

Sandy noticed that Turtle had a decent ability with chord
changes.

"Let me hear what you know," Sandy told her, while
the downstairs emptied reliably into the room around them.

Well, that would be Melissa Etheridge; Turtle cleared her
throat and launched into "All the Way to Heaven," the
scabby blue turtle popping in and out of view as she slid
her left hand up and down the neck of the instrument.

In many ways it was a very ordinary teenage Saturday,
hours sliding by in a circle of good friends and deferred
love interests, with Turtle at the center. The live music eventually gave way to a Grateful Dead cd.

There was a lot more drinking than usual, however, on
this particular night. Stacey was sober as a nun and acutely
attentive to her friends' needs, fetching ice water for
Sandy's headache and worrying at Dana, whose strep throat
and runny nose were making her miserable and even fever-
ish by now. But by 2:00, the 18-pack was almost gone, and
the beer had helped loosen the persistent edginess among
the drinkers into something more explosive.

Turtle managed to get Sandy alone in her bedroom, with
bold plans to confront her rival. Instead, the real action was

down at the other end of the hall, between the bodies now sprawled on Robyn's bed.

First, there was the kind of boozey moment that these sexually experienced but hardly orgiastic girls weren't accustomed to: Tracy had a bag of sugar that they had brought up from Stephanie's to make Kool-Aid with, and she was putting little piles of it on her tongue and kissing everybody. Robyn's bed became "the Sugar Room" and Tracy started a trail of kisses. She kissed Stephanie, Stephanie kissed Dana, Dana kissed Stacey—and Stacey kissed Tracy.

And then Tracy broke down in tears.

Nobody had ever seen Tracy cry before. But then nobody had ever seen her this drunk. "I love Turtle," she sobbed, her big face shiny with tears. "I *love* her. I don't love Sandy. I don't *want* to be with Sandy."

Dana, Stephanie, and Stacey listened quietly. There was nothing to say, really. But now Sandy was leaving, and Tracy was about to follow her dutifully downstairs.

Turtle was standing in the hallway when Tracy walked past.

"I'm gonna do it right now," Tracy told her.

"What are you talking about?"

"Don't worry about it," is all she said before the stairs turned and she was gone. But the message was clear: Tracy was going to break up with Sandy and everything was going to be okay.

Too bad for Turtle that Stacey was there in the hallway too, the proverbial fly on the wall, to ruin her cheer.

"Do you know what she's gonna go do?" Stacey asked Turtle now, following her back to her room and her guitar.

"Yeah, she's gonna go break up with her."

"No, she's gonna go tell her that she loves her. She wants to be with her. She doesn't want to have anything to do with you, and she's gonna try to break it to you lightly."

"W-w-what?"

Turtle's resistance to this story was wearing thin by now.

This latest accounting went on and on and she just couldn't think straight. So she listened.

"She was just in there saying that she's gonna ask her to marry her," Stacey told her. "She said that she's basically using you for a place to live, and you pay her rent, and, you know."

Turtle didn't want to hear any more. She threw her guitar pick at the wall and stormed out, slamming the door behind her. "Just go away, Stacey!" she shouted on her way downstairs. "Leave me *alone!*"

Turtle would just have to see for herself. Maybe Tracy *was* trying to pull one over on her. Maybe this time Stacey was right. And sure enough, when she looked out the front door of the house, there they were—Sandy and the love of Turtle's life—holding each other on the sidewalk!

Turtle propelled herself, fuming, over to the refrigerator. She was pulling out another beer when the phone rang: Robyn was off work and ready for a ride home. Sandy and her pickup pulled away from the curb just then, and Tracy appeared in the doorway.

When their eyes met, Turtle knew what she had to do. She was a strategic warrior. She would let Tracy know how angry she was, any minute now, but she wasn't conceding defeat. Sandy had gone home, hadn't she? For now, Tracy belonged to Turtle.

"You wanna ride with us to get Robyn?" she asked Tracy.

"Yeah, Boo," came the answer.

If Tracy was a little vague about what was coming, Sandy seems to have her head fully in the sand. Not only did she fail to guess at Tracy's wandering heart but, as far as she was concerned, there was nothing brewing with any of them.

"I saw nothing," she would say. "That was the weird part. I was like, Hold on, they were so happy there! No anger whatsoever. Nobody was pissed at anybody. Turtle wasn't mad. And Tracy didn't give a hoot."

* * *

A drunken Domica showed up again just in time to stumble into the Tempo with Turtle, Tracy, and Stephanie, who plowed Thompson Street at her usual, accelerated pace and then turned left onto stately old Monument Avenue just west of the new Arthur Ashe statue.

The truth began to trickle out as Turtle and Tracy fought, connected the dots, made up, and whipped themselves into a whole new fury. The ride to Willow Lawn was just the ten minutes they needed to reach a tremulous peak of rage.

"You said you loved me?" Turtle marveled. "Well that's not what Stacey said."

"I can't believe it. Fuck that girl!"

"I just wanna fuckin' beat her ass," Turtle went on.

Stephanie pulled up in front of Ruby Tuesday. And Robyn, climbing into the back seat of the car, received a wet kiss, tongue and all, from shy Domica. "Oh my God, how much have you had to drink?" Robyn gasped, realizing as she asked this that Tracy and Turtle were plastered too.

Plastered, furious about something, and in love again, from the looks of it.

"We're going to kick Stacey's fucking ass," Tracy told her.

"Yup," echoed Turtle.

Turtle now gave Robyn a blow-by-blow account that managed to confuse her completely. But the big picture was quite clear. "Everyone in that car was mad at Stacey," Robyn would remember. Domica helped with an occasional "Yeah" and Stephanie was sober and serious, but solidly behind them too.

"You know you need to get that girl outta your house," Stephanie advised, taking her eyes off the road and turning around for emphasis. "'Cause she's just manipulating every single one of you."

Then suddenly there was a plan, with specifics that seemed to materialize on their own: They were going to take Stacey outside somewhere where her screams couldn't be heard—and teach her a lesson.

"I know the perfect spot," Tracy said. Behind the Chesterfield County Airport, down near where she grew up. A place called Marsh Field.

Those were Stephanie's old stomping grounds too, but she'd never heard of this Marsh Field.

"Don't worry, I'll get you there," Tracy told her.

Now all they had to do was get Stacey.

"No beer? Fuck you."

Five bucks and enough forethought to mention it in the middle of the afternoon and once again, Robyn's house was dry. Tracy climbed the stairs, and Turtle tried to get Robyn off of the bad beer situation and interested in Marsh Field.

"Hey," Domica asked Turtle quietly from that black lacquered table in the dining room, where she was holding a hugga-hugga orange boxcutter in each hand. "Which one of these is sharper?"

"We can't *kill* the girl," Turtle muttered on her way upstairs. Robyn followed, slammed her own bedroom door behind her, and resisted a wave of entreaties from the hallway.

"No, I gotta work in the morning," she told them.

Stacey, who was all ready for bed in Turtle's room, was also resisting.

"We're just going to go for a drive," Turtle pleaded.

"It'll be fun," said Tracy. "A family outing."

"I'll come if Dana comes," Stacey announced. And she was so insistent about it that you have to wonder what she knew, or felt in her bones. Probably she reasoned that nothing bad would happen with Dana there, that she was thwarting anything nefarious they might have planned for her.

Domica would guess later that Stacey was clueless about what was to come. "We always go somewhere and just do a big bonding thing," she said. "So she thought it was gonna be a bonding thing." But Domica had polished off something like ten beers and a wine cooler by now and her judgment wouldn't have been very good.

Robyn was genuinely in the dark, or so she has said. "I

honestly thought it was all talk. I really believed that they were just talkin'."

In the end, Dana agreed to come even though she was feeling so sick. She said she didn't want to be home alone, or at least alone with Robyn fuming. So Stacey went too, wearing Turtle's blue Champion basketball shorts with the white waistband folded over and a white T-shirt that said "We Hate Her!" She wasn't wearing a bra because she had already removed it for the night, but she had on the green watch she had given Turtle. There was some tying of shoes, although Stacey stayed barefoot. Tracy wore a pair of sports sandals. And Turtle wore Tracy's hat—the white one with the plaid brim, the one that had "Sandy" penned on the back.

There are big leaps to make between a "bonding thing," an "ass-kicking," and a murder. But the ball was now rolling. Two of the boxcutters were discreetly pocketed on the way out the door; the third one stayed behind.

PART THREE

Baby Faces

"Someone posed the question to me: 'Had it been Stacey with these girls, all of them ganging up on, say, Domica, would Stacey have backed away?' Who knows? I would hope so. Dear God, I would hope so. But I just don't believe that your upbringing leads you to this kind of thing. I have seen kids who have been raped for 20 years and tortured. They don't grow up to murder people."

—Debbie Parker, social worker

8:

"I'm the strong one. I'm the one that's supposed to
be fucking butch. I'm the one that doesn't fucking cry.
I'm the one that gets the last word in everything."
                                                    —Turtle

Gillian Anderson, the redhead who plays solemn Dana
Scully on "The X-Files," had blue turtles tattooed onto her
ankles because they're a Tahitian symbol for peace of mind.
For Kelley Tibbs, it was more of a talisman. A Pueblo In-
dian once told her that she had the soul of a turtle—it had
already been her grandmother's refrain that she was as slow
as one—and pretty soon she had a turtle inscribed in green
and blue on her left forearm. Turtle items piled up quickly
as gifts, including several live ones that may still roam the
spaces between the walls at 210 South Belmont.

The tattoo helped clinch the nickname, but it was also
that Turtle quite insisted upon it—Turtle's mom Doris, Robyn, and ex-girlfriend Sarah Franklin were the only ones
allowed to call her Kelley. (She also strongly preferred
"Lee" as a middle name to the "Ann" on her birth certificate.)

Reproducing Turtle's personal mark that Saturday afternoon with their own sharp inscriptions of blue ink was probably something of a sacrificial offering from her friends. If
Turtle was the "ringleader" of this group, as the newspa-
pers would trumpet later on, it was because the force of her
personality put her at the center of every circle she touched.

That is, once she got the hang of fighting her own bad odds, a battle she started very early in life.

As Turtle was growing up, her mother had work most of the time at one branch or another of the same restaurant chain. Later she ran a topless bar called Twin Peaks. Home moved around between boyfriends with unfriendly families and boyfriends who liked to talk to little Turtle about sex.

What a relief, when Turtle was 10, that she could go live at the Renaissance Center retirement home with her great-grandmother and inject her with insulin in the mornings; Turtle was devastated by the old woman's death that next year. At 12, Turtle infuriated her mom by announcing that she was gay, and went to live for a while with Diane Posenough, the older lesbian in the trailer next door. Diane made her get up every morning and go to sixth grade—and took her back into her home later that year when Kelley got into some really big trouble:

In the summer of 1991, Diane was working the cash register at an East Coast convenience store up on Broad Rock Road, and Turtle would traipse up there in the dark sometimes, just to hang out. It wasn't the safest late-night journey for a young girl to make, alone and on foot, but this was mild little Chesterfield County.

On the way back one night, five boys chased her into the parking lot of a Ukrop's grocery store and took turns raping her. The ending would be all too haunting six summers later: the boys discarded Turtle afterwards in a mud puddle. Marisa was born nine months after that.

At 14, Turtle devoted herself to the care of her grandmother, the woman who had meant the most to her so far in her life. No one was around the day she finally succumbed to cancer, so Turtle gave her mouth-to-mouth resuscitation while infant Marisa looked on from the other side of the room.

If Turtle's rape helped toughen her, losing her grandmother got to her soft center: She was so horrified that she tried to kill herself by washing down a handful of asthma pills and downers with a stiff drink—and then cutting her wrist. Doris threw her in the shower and sent her to an outpatient counselor the next day.

Turtle has always been better with people than books. She never really learned to read—the diagnosis was dyslexia, and then "slow learner." She barely finished 6th grade, and failed an attempt at summer school several years later. By then, though, Doris's latest guy was making persistent advances, and she went off to find the world out of Michael Hicks' Sheppard Street living room. Marisa was mostly with Doris after that, and although she was not the most attentive of grandmas, Turtle's distance was not entirely bad for Marisa. She had some growing up of her own to do.

There was nothing Michael wouldn't do for Turtle Tibbs, and she was always at the ready with requests, whether "Mike, can I have a beer?" or "Mike, can I have a $500 check to pay Robyn the money I owe her?"

The pool table he had set up in the front room of the Sheppard Street house was definitely not about having guys over from the office for a game. It was for Turtle; when she wasn't around, it was for mail and coats. Her room at Michael's, with its black-and-white paint-splattered walls and glow-in-the-dark stars on the ceiling, would always be ready for her.

Turtle was hardly in a position to complain about his inability to rise above despite the resources at his disposal: His house, surrounded by quaint Victorian porches and within reach of young Richmond's favorite Carytown brunches and wine stores, would have been worth a lot of money if it weren't falling down around his ears. And he made a good living as an engineer.

Robyn, on the other hand, found it annoying. "Sixty thousand bucks in his checking account alone and he can't pay his gas and water bill," she snorted.

In any case, Michael was no father; Turtle didn't know her real dad, but probably would have selected Jon Klein, a ROSMY counselor, as a replacement. Turtle's best guide has always been ROSMY itself, though, where she was one of the first members back in 1993. "Some people go to church. She went to ROSMY," Sarah Franklin would try to explain.

"I was home—I had a place to belong," Turtle was quoted as saying about ROSMY in a 1996 newsletter. "The meetings gave me people and a place that stayed the same, like an anchor, when everything else was changing."

9:

"Everybody knows I'm a buncha talkin'."

—Tracy

Standing out in a crowd isn't good for adolescent girls. Tracy's great height won her a prized place on the varsity basketball team from ninth grade on, but off the court, she was self-conscious about looming over other people. Friends lost track of her childhood warmth somewhere behind the hokey shag haircut and the bulky glasses. In high school, Tracy was expected to be a bully because she was so big, and sometimes she found it easiest to act like one. People kept their distance in class, on the bus, in the locker room.

Tracy's friendly side would take some coddling to bring back. And that wasn't forthcoming at home, especially after her half-brother Daniel was born. Tracy was 15. And while Daniel would become the most important thing in her life— surpassing even basketball, and later karate—she came to miss her mother's attention, lately on the wane anyway since her marriage to Daniel's father, Lee Seward.

Mostly what Tracy felt was left out: The day her mother gave birth, she stayed all day at her bedside. But on the last night of the hospital stay, her mom and dad and baby brother ate dinner in the cafeteria and Tracy would remember with searing frustration that she wasn't allowed in at all—only the parents.

Then one afternoon the summer after her junior year, Tracy was fetching her brother from his babysitter when she noticed two pretty, blond, identical-twin sisters playing tennis. She recognized Danielle Felice as an ex-boyfriend's current squeeze.

On her way back home with two-year-old Daniel, she noticed they were still playing and decided to speak up.

"Hey, Danielle!" Tracy shouted across the court.

"Hey, Tracy!"

The trio quickly made friends. Danielle and Tracy had Biology together that year, and sister Karla's class was next door. The twins took the big step of switching lunch tables so they could sit with Tracy.

"It's kind of a package deal," Karla would explain later. "Almost all our friends are, like, shared."

They all took up karate, and Danielle and Tracy got serious enough to travel for tournaments. Weekends, they would join a swarm of friends at the movies or down at one of the beaches on the James River: Pony Pasture, Brown's Island, Belle Isle.

Tracy wouldn't meet Turtle until later, but it's likely that they crossed paths on one of those riverbanks sometime in '95 or '96. Or maybe on that walkway suspended under the Lee Bridge, where Tracy and the twins would bring their fishing poles when they skipped school.

Tracy seemed happier that last year of high school, and certainly she was more contented with herself. She clipped off the tails of hair down her back—her "redneck" hairdo, as Karla liked to tease—and got contacts.

And then she fell in love with Karla.

It was the first lesbian relationship for both—not that either of them felt that their passion had anything to do with being gay. Tracy insisted that there would never be another girl: There was trouble if Karla suggested it.

"I'm not gay," Tracy would correct her.

"You're gay."

"I'm not fucking gay!" Tracy was enraged.

"Calm down."

They kept their romance quite secret from their families;

they were best friends as far as their parents knew. Then one day, an incriminating love note came into the wrong hands. Karla was banished from Tracy's home, and a long, difficult period of conflict followed. Tracy's mother was not prepared to accept a gay daughter; it was the influence on Daniel that seemed to worry her most.

Eventually Tracy was told to leave, and she moved into her grandmother's trailer—over at Green Leigh, coincidentally, a matter of feet from the home of her future friend, Stephanie Cull. Karla joined her there for a while when her family's condo burned to the ground in an accident.

Those were hard times for Tracy. She talked about joining the military, but she didn't want to leave Karla. Mostly, though, she was obsessed with finding a way back to her mother's home.

"There were walls built there," Karla would say about that. "What her mother really wanted was Daniel, Lee, and herself. Tracy wasn't anywhere in that equation. And it hurt Tracy so much."

Meanwhile, Karla was starting to have trouble with Tracy's temper. They had their own quarrels, but it was behind the wheel of a car that Tracy could be scariest. One day, with Karla and two friends watching from the Taurus, she got into a fight on the shoulder of a highway with two girls who had pulled out in front of her in their car. Tracy had the upper hand from the start and sent them running for their lives. But the next week, she tried it again—with the wrong people.

Tracy and Karla were leaving the parking lot at a state fair when a carful of teenage boys and girls indicated that Tracy's car was blocking their exit. Tracy motioned for them to go around, but when the traffic opened up, they stayed on her tail, pelting the car with garbage and making graphic threats.

At first, Tracy was level-headed about it. She monitored the situation quietly in the rear-view mirror and told Karla,

"Stay calm." But then she seemed to wind herself into a rage. It must have been the success of the week before that compelled Tracy to pull off onto the side of the road and climb right under a shower of fists. When Karla ran into the fray to try and help, she was knocked to the ground and pummeled. They were lucky that their assailants didn't have guns. "I've got your license-plate number!" Karla yelled from the ground as they finally sauntered back to their car and sped off.

At the gas station where the girls went to phone the police, Tracy was repentant. What had she done to her sweet lover, her best friend?

"Don't break up with me!" Tracy pleaded. "I love you. I'm *so* sorry. Oh my God, I almost lost you!"

Karla was okay when the shock wore off, and she forgave Tracy right away. But she was beginning to be afraid of her pugnacious girlfriend. Especially as their own arguments grew more frequent. Her parents—even her sister—told her they didn't trust Tracy, worried that she might hurt Karla. Once, the couple was fighting in Danielle's car and Tracy busted the windshield in a fury.

Karla split up with Tracy not long after that incident. It was the fall of 1996. The breakup was hard enough on Tracy, but Karla began dating a guy named Michael who forbade her to see Tracy at all—part jealousy, part homophobia, as Karla saw it.

Eventually Karla would see Tracy in secret; Tracy hung onto her friendship with the twins even as she started spending time with Turtle and a whole slew of young lesbians up in Richmond.

In the spring of 1997, the twins sometimes came around to South Belmont Avenue. Karla even got to know Turtle a little bit. But they didn't really approve, especially when they realized that Tracy was starting to drink and had completely stopped doing karate.

"She wasn't happy with herself," says Karla. "She wasn't doing anything with her life. She was partying all the time. She totally regressed from what she had become.

It was so odd. It just really hurt us to see her like that.

"I guess she had gotten so involved with these people and, you know, the nightlife and the excitement of it all. But when she woke up in the morning, where she wanted to be was at home."

10:

"This is the first time I've ever been violent. 'Cause usually when I get into fights I don't fight back. I usually let the people just . . . beat me."

—Domica

At 9:30 every Saturday morning between September and March, for as many years as anyone can remember, three generations of Wincklers bowled at Schrader Lanes, an old white stucco building set back from the immense shopping centers of Richmond's West End. Domica's grandfather Frank, a slight, softspoken man, was a big scorer. So was his son from a second marriage, Jajuan, who was around Domica's age. Then there was usually Domica's mom, Pam, and her sister's son Ricky. Domica was no star, but she could pick up an occasional spare. In any case, it was a commitment that the Wincklers seemed to take seriously. They were always done by lunch.

Jajuan stayed on at Schrader's into high school. And Frank played now and then. But by the time Domica was 13, her thoughts were elsewhere. Would that it were something good—school, a romance—keeping her away.

But that was '92–93, the year her mother went to jail for six months for embezzlement, her cousin Chiquita got 20 years for the murder of her infant child, and her Great-Uncle Carl died of AIDS. Domica, an only child, was reeling from all that—and from the fact that nobody explained any of it to her—when her mother announced that she was sending her to live with her father and his new wife. According to the social history commissioned by Domica's defense attorneys, her stepmother had a history of turning her father against her.

Domica decided, *No way, not that again.* She jotted down some goodbyes, swallowed nearly 50 Bayer aspirins, and passed out. Her cousin Benita found the suicide note. Domica spent several days recovering at Richmond's Medical College of Virginia Hospital.

You could say it was a really bad year, but there had been so many in Domica's young life. She herself was never a sparkler. Her mother sent her to counseling in elementary school for being so quiet—although that might have had something to do with changing schools five times before eighth grade while trailing her mother's boyfriends all around the state (one of whom molested Domica when she was in fourth grade).

That counseling was one of the very few times that anyone showed concern about Domica's tendency to withdraw—not just from pain but from emotional situations of any kind. In part, because her behavior was merely at the most extreme end of the family norm: The Wincklers were not big talkers.

Both parents found lovers who were jealous of Domica. But Michael Davis's wife Bonnie pretty much made him choose—it was either her or the kid.

The first sign of trouble was when Domica was six and dropped from their wedding at the last minute because she didn't have the right shoes. Disappointment would be the theme; her dad almost never called or wrote, and when he did, there were promises made—and mostly broken. One year he placed a pile of Christmas gifts on layaway and never retrieved them. The night before a long-planned vacation at Virginia Beach, somebody figured out that there wouldn't be enough room for Domica after all.

Domica also endured humiliation of the physical sort. When she was a wispy nine, she visited her father's new family in Georgia and one night helped her step-brother

Mikey sneak a cookie. The next day, Bonnie summoned her from the bathroom and tore into her with the sharp edge of a leather belt. Another time, Mikey reported that Domica was threatening him, and Bonnie latched onto Domica's throat and needed to be pried away.

None of this seemed to provoke a reaction, to prompt Domica to take out her pain on weaker kids, for example. Rather, her behavior was to the other extreme. Cousins, teachers, and classmates watched her cower before tormentors all her life. A neighbor called her a "scaredy cat." In fact, she attracted bullies consistently, and it was only in high school that there was any kind of explanation.

Domica drew all the wrong kind of attention at Thomas Jefferson High. She slept around, and the guys were usually taken—by female schoolmates who then tracked her down and beat her up without fail. There seemed less and less of a reason to make the trip up there every day from the Carytown house at 3110 Parkwood Avenue where she lived with her mother, her Aunt Francine, and Ricky and Benita.

By the time Domica's mother gave birth to her little sister Shamica in March of 1996, Domica was failing most subjects and skipping class every day. Pam agreed to let her drop out to take care of the baby, and she quit her job at Shoney's restaurant, where Domica had worked part-time for years.

Domica met up with the South Belmont girls around the corner that next year, and right away there were changes. Part of it was a teenager's natural hunger for personal style, new meaning—and Domica's apparent interest in experimenting with girls. She cut her hair super-short, started to dress differently, and was toying with attractions to both Robyn and Turtle.

But neighbors and family noticed that she seemed bothered by something. She had already learned to put away a lot of beer and now she drank even more. Certainly, she had not an ounce of initiative in her body. One day in late July, Domica got beaten up by a neighborhood girl on her own doorstep. As the neighbor may have been expecting, she didn't lift a finger in her own defense.

"Domica was like a zombie," the mother of a friend would remember about that period of time. "She was so neutralized it was scary. I was afraid for her."

11:

"They were the first gay people I met. It was cool around people who not only accepted me but were like me. 'Cause at school I was always cast out."
—Stephanie

Stephanie Cull was a happy, dimpled two-year-old when her knees swelled up the first time. Her mom Cindy, a heavyset, no-nonsense Kansan, applied ice at the recommendation of the family doctor. Within weeks the little girl was diagnosed with pediatric rheumatoid arthritis and stepping up to painkillers and steroids.

In the photographs that Cindy would later pin up in her office at the Medical College of Virginia, Stephanie is playful and grinning on her second birthday, her hair pulled into a silky topknot. At the end of that year, her hair now clipped into a blunt, boyish bowl, the natural downturn of her lips is evident and something serious has happened to her eyes.

Stephanie's joints screamed most days after that. Sometimes she couldn't get out of bed at all or sit upright for meals with the foursome who shared her cozy shoebox home on the easternmost edge of Green Leigh trailer park: her mother, her grandmother, her brother Chris, and her cousin Derek, both a decade her senior. The only thing worse than the pain was the unpredictability of her symptoms: A flareup could keep her in a wheelchair one day and be mysteriously, blessedly, gone the next—and the kids at school didn't understand. Not only was she a freak, they figured, maybe she was faking it too.

Stephanie's arthritis went into remission at one point. But then in 7th grade, a 16-year-old putting a cassette tape into her car stereo ran a red light and smashed into a car that Cindy's best friend was driving—with Stephanie in the back seat. Stephanie's knees were badly smashed, and the arthritis was jolted back to life. They might have sued, but Stephanie chose not to testify. They settled out of court for $20,000, half of which she would pocket at 16 and half at 18.

Stephanie's physical problems were exacerbated by the shyness she had inherited from her mother. Another child might have better handled the teasing and the fuss about gym class; another child would have made more friends. But Cindy was also the best thing she had going. If Stephanie was a little slow about growing up because of their bond, with Cindy always there to bring her anything that was out of reach, she also made sure that she didn't stop reaching. In junior high, Cindy coaxed her baby-faced daughter into the Girl Scouts and signed herself up to lead the troop. Except for some extra hanging around the campfire, Stephanie kept up.

The other early certainty about Stephanie was that she liked girls. She was captivated by her kindergarten teacher from the moment "Miss Angel" carried her fragile charge piggyback-style from the school building during a fire drill. Way into junior high, Stephanie was still stopping by to see how Miss Angel was getting along. By then, though, female classmates were just as interesting. "Damn, there's something weird going on, 'cause I like boys *and* girls," she told a friend.

It would only get weirder at Byrd High, a flat, sprawling maze located in a richer area of Chesterfield County where Stephanie had to be bused because all the schools closer-by had stairs. Stephanie tried mixing at first, dressing the varsity part, showing up at football games. But she was drawn to the bad kids, first as a follower and then with the ferocity of a natural trendsetter.

Pretty soon, Stephanie had shaved the sides of her head, dyed the tufty mohawk on the crown of her head a bright blue, and started shrugging around school in a black leather motorcycle jacket. She also let it be known that she had a crush on a girl named Michelle. For all the sheltered kiddies at Byrd High, Stephanie was "the bi girl with blue hair."

The adults around her would wonder how much this bold explosion of personality had to do with the trauma of nearly losing her mother to a stroke that year. Stephanie was on her own in a way that she had never been before. But the problem was that punks and "bi girls"—and "yo girls" later, when Stephanie introduced hip-hop pants—were not only unheard of at Byrd but distinctly unwelcome.

One classmate was rather intrigued, though. In January 1996, the middle of Stephanie's junior year, she had a birthday party at a local pizza restaurant and a senior named Claire Watson, whom she knew as her friend Wesley's ex-girlfriend, came along. They got to chatting, and Claire threw her a curve ball.

"So you wanna go to Pyramid with me to check out chicks?" Claire asked, and Stephanie could only gulp with amazement. Claire? Chicks? The Pyramid was a gay bar up in Richmond!

They did check out chicks there, the very next evening, but they only had eyes for each other.

Then one icy night in February, Stephanie and Claire took a drive with friends to King's Dominion, an amusement park north of Richmond that Paramount, the movie company, ran on an Old South theme (the rollercoaster is called the Rebel Yell). Claire drove with Stephanie's head in her lap. Later, they stretched out side-by-side on the hood of the car, their breath freezing into romantic little puffs over their heads.

"Is it okay if I put my arm around you?" Stephanie inquired.

Oh yeah, Claire was fine with that.

That was about as far as it got that night, neither being the type to lean in confidently for a kiss. But in a matter of days, they were Byrd High's first "out" lesbian couple—a scary proposition to say the least:

It was 1996. Happy gay films from the outside world were making it into Chesterfield County; Stephanie and Claire saw *The Incredibly True Adventure of Two Girls in Love* and *Go Fish*. But there was bad news too. Real, live, openly gay small-town teenagers were enduring schoolyard bashings all over the country, at places just like Byrd.

The couple's mere holding of hands could still an entire hallway of classmates; when they dared cross the lunch room together it was under a shower of catcalls and stupid questions: "Do you really have sex?" "How can you do that?" "What do your parents think?" And to Stephanie— almost every day, and sometimes with her back pushed up against a locker—"What are you exactly? A boy or a girl?"

Being a couple never got easier, and the harassment took its toll. After some months of it, Byrd High became a scary place for Stephanie and Claire. By the time a troop of frenzied girls followed them into a school bathroom by means of a warning, the two had just about stopped showing up for class. Nobody got touched in the bathroom incident, but it was made clear that that was next.

A school guidance counselor figured that the pestering wouldn't have such a sting if they met other gay people their age—at ROSMY, maybe, the youth group up in Richmond.

But then Stephanie got mononucleosis right before spring break and was out sick for so long that Byrd arranged for home schooling at her kitchen table. There was no way she was going back. She swore to her mother that she'd get her GED, and Cindy gave her the green light to drop out. Claire joined her, kind of unofficially. She was graduating, and her springtime fadeout went without a lot of notice.

It was tempting to make an appearance together at Claire's senior prom, however. So they did. Above their nearly identical suede sneakers, their outfits were a study in butch and femme. Stephanie—her head still shaved all around the sides but that top layer reaching her shoulders now—wore a tuxedo with a black bow tie and a tiny loop in her right nostril. Claire wore a white, shiny Japanese-style dress, her long brown hair curling at the ends. A white corsage decorated her left wrist.

High school hell was behind them when they finally took that counselor's advice and checked out ROSMY one summer Saturday. They were scared to death. Fifteen or 20 teenagers were standing outside smoking cigarettes, holding sodas, chatting knowingly. They all seemed so much older and more experienced, especially in love.

Eventually an adult showed up and had them choose partners for an exercise that involved planning a "Perfect 24 Hours." Stephanie's partner was Turtle Tibbs. She was just about the coolest one there, and she also had a lot in common with Stephanie: a passion for the Grateful Dead and a lifelong obsession with Winnie-the-Pooh, among other things. They breezed through the exercise; their perfect day involved adopting a pet lizard or snake and going to the beach and getting high.

Stephanie and Claire went to ROSMY again in the fall to get application forms for an AIDS demonstration they had heard about. A local high school was inviting ROSMY kids to go along on the bus with them to Washington. The famous AIDS Quilt would be on display for the last time, and there was going to be a rally on the steps of the Capitol about legalizing needle exchange: the practice of giving heroin addicts clean needles to stop the spread of the HIV virus.

The excitement of that trip was worth 100 ROSMY exercises. "It was the first time any of us had been a part of anything like that," says Claire. She and Stephanie marched around Washington alongside Turtle and her posse with their heads in the clouds.

Of course, all that power and pride got the love juices flowing too. The flirting was out of control, especially between Stephanie and Turtle. Turtle's girlfriend Melissa joined Claire in her disgust. They sat next to each other on the bus trip back to Richmond and stewed.

PART FOUR

Blood in the Grass

"It wasn't intentional that they caused Stacey to suffer for so long. It's that they don't know what to do. Bit by bit they're escalating. And they're really inept at killing her."

—Evan Nelson, forensic psychologist

12:

In the late 1980s, Walter Marsh bought six acres of woods on the western edge of the quiet little Chesterfield airport and set about building a personal garage and airplane hangar. Marsh was a pilot with a fascination for watching planes take off and land, and a mechanical engineer with a tireless tinkering gene.

The problem was that there were laws against building a garage without a house. So Marsh got two pigs, named them Orville and Wilbur after the Wright brothers, cut down some trees, and put up a corrugated aluminum farm building—farm structures being exempt from the building code. He hauled the material around on a pair of antique yellow fire trucks that he picked up for $1,000. (He also paraded his family in them at fairs, and even won a trophy.)

The inside of his new "farm building" was a mechanical wonderland. At one point, there were three airplanes, two motorcyles, a tractor, an airport tug, two trailers, a forklift truck, and a couple of drill presses and lathes. "I don't think he ever grew out of the Tonka toy stage," his wife Charlotte would comment.

Marsh ran a machine company called Retrofit Controls of Virginia. When he wasn't fixing engines or trying to grade his rough, stumpy six acres into something resembling a pasture, he was over at the airport's main hangar with other distinguished members of the Chesterfield Pilot's Association.

Hangars are constructed so that planes can line up together in two long rows, with their noses facing outward and their tails alternating in the spaces between. At each end, there's an L-shaped space that stands empty—basically the size of half a plane. It was in one of these that the Association established a pilots' lounge, a drinking and dining club where they'd meet in the evenings to catch up on local aeronautic activities.

And to complain.

The cyclone fence that the new airport manager had put up on the airfield's periphery was a favorite beef. The airport had to be enclosed to get FAA funding, but the fence cut off access for lots of folks, including Walter Marsh. How was he supposed to get his planes out onto the runway? The industrial park on the airport's eastern flank, which had been growing into something of a hub in the early '90s with the participation of big companies like Reynolds Metal Co., was also cut off. One company sued for breach of contract—and won.

Eventually, the pilots' club itself came up against the unfriendly airport manager. The new guy didn't like the club or their cocktails, and the Association was sent packing. Thank God for Marsh Field.

The pigs had long ago gone to sausage when Walter came up with his next scheme. The county said, This is no farm, and so he went the personal garage route. He set up a combination office and dwelling inside the hangar, and dubbed the windowless cavern around it an "attached garage."

It was a warehouse, by all other definitions. And on Tuesday nights, it was the relocated Pilot's Association club—greatly improved a year and a half later by a runway-view "deck" (in building-permit terms), a 40-foot tower with a zig-zag of stairs that Marsh put up over by the airport fence. There was a picnic table up there, and the pilots would sip mint juleps on warm summer evenings and watch students land—a boisterous Olympic scoring committee, quite in the manner of men enjoying their leisure time but dead serious at the same time.

A sign down at the front end of the driveway announced "Marsh Field."

It was all very nice, just the playground that Marsh had intended. Charlotte planted a garden with supplies purchased on their daughter's summer job discount at Southern States. And one of the pilots kept the fruit and vegetables watered and weeded, out there in the field, away from the warehouse, where the sun hit it year-round.

On weekends, the field was becoming a late-night parking spot for teenagers, but Marsh had no trouble with that—at first. He'd drive up on a Saturday, see some darkened vehicle out there in the field, wander over, and knock on the window.

"You know, I don't care if you come here or not," he'd tell them. "Just don't leave no trash, don't start no fires."

Those were his rules. He genuinely didn't mind the parking itself, even when his daughter came home from high school one day and announced, "I was in the cafeteria line and some of the kids were saying, 'There's a place to go.' And I realized we owned it."

Early in the summer of 1997, however, somebody was getting rowdy. Marsh would drive up on a Sunday morning and stumble into beer cans; sometimes there was spray paint on his walls and signs, or tomatoes had been plucked from the garden and smashed about. The kids were also climbing the tower and throwing beer cans onto the roof of the warehouse. When their sport opened a hole up there, Marsh contacted the Chesterfield County police about checking on the place late Fridays and Saturdays. And when the vandals threw the picnic table right off the tower, Walter Marsh's famous patience cracked.

By the week of the murder, he was taking the criminal-chasing as seriously as any other project: Sometimes he was up there at 2 in the morning himself, trying out new techniques for catching the vandals. He wired up some security lights so they would go on inside the hangar when anybody drove onto the property; the trespassers couldn't see the lights from outside. The idea was to get on the phone to police the moment the lights switched on.

* * *

On Saturday, July 26th, Walter and Charlotte caught a film at the Genito Forest Cinema with a couple of their kids. On the way back home, they stopped off at Marsh Field to check the garden for cantaloupes. They'd been great that season, amazingly sweet, and Charlotte was keen on finding a couple of ripe ones for Sunday breakfast.

They pulled in at about ten and right away noticed a white pickup parked over by the warehouse: Might a group of paint-toting hoodlums be lurking around back by the tower? Not tonight. Walter recognized the truck as belonging to Denny Harrison, a friend who sometimes crashed inside. And there he was, asleep on the couch when they went in for a flashlight.

The headlights of the car further illuminated the field, where the Marsh family poked around in the shadows and noticed that it had rained there earlier; the northern part of the county where they lived had stayed dry.

There were several nice melons and they carried these back to the car. They were too early to find anything else.

13:

"How bizarre! How bizarre!"

The words screeched at full-volume from the speakers in Stephanie's car, where Turtle rode—dancing, somehow—on Tracy's lap. "How bizarre! How bizarre!" the song repeated.

The city was way behind them now, and the entire front seat seemed uplifted by the journey south. But not so the back.

Dana, bent over and miserable behind Stephanie, had just added nausea to her long list of symptoms by swallowing a sleeping pill—and then losing most of it again on the pavement a few miles back. Domica sulked at the other window. And Stacey, in the middle, was suffering her severest attack of invisibility yet—at the very moment, tragically, that she was utmost on *almost* everyone's mind.

Dana was still unaware of the plan.

They were looking for Cogbill Road, the pretty, tree-lined road that, had they been making a left, would have taken them to Meadowbrook High and the gymnasium of Tracy's more athletic days. The Felice twins lived right across the street from the school; now they slept.

But the Tempo would be going right, where Cogbill headed west between an East Coast convenience store and a 7-Eleven. When this corner came into view, Tracy had to speak up because the music was so loud.

"Turn right," she barked.

Pretty soon the all-night, neon glow had melted into a dark, densely wooded residential stretch. The song was over now, and Stephanie turned the radio down so that she could hear what Tracy was saying.

"It's somewhere up here," Tracy told her, as the houses got fewer on the right and the Heritage Baptist Church flew by on the left.

The Tempo finally left the pavement at a white picket fence that looked like the entrance to a farm. A sign out front read "Marsh Field."

They bounced up into a clearing and came to a stop next to a warehouse on the right. There was a white pickup by the building, a picnic table in a field of grass, and beyond that, a tower with stairs and the tall cyclone fence of the Chesterfield airport. A sparkle of runway lights illuminated the area just slightly, and there was a small fluorescent bulb over the warehouse door. But no one in sight.

"I'm staying in the car with you," Stacey whispered to Dana as the others disappeared into the night. And for a few minutes, it was just the two of them in the car. Then Turtle was back.

"Okay," she said, opening the back door. "*I*'m sitting with Joe."

"Are you sure?" Stacey asked.

"Yeah, go ahead."

Outside, leaning against the car, Domica was speaking with Stephanie about the boxcutter in her pocket. Stephanie handed it over.

Then Stacey was out in the open air too and Dana was being briefed in the back seat.

"You know how Tracy was saying, you know, 'I love Turtle'?" Turtle asked her.

"Yeah, I know, I was there."

"Well Stacey came to me and said that, um, that Tracy *didn't* love me, that she didn't want to be with me, that she wanted to be with Sandy."

Turtle paused here.

Dana said nothing.

"So, well, we gotta kick her ass."

* * *

When Turtle left Dana alone in the car, Stephanie was sitting at the picnic table; the arthritis made it hard for her to stand around or fold her legs under her on the ground. Stacey herself was fully seated in the grass, barefoot and oblivious. She gazed out at the runway with her back to the car, to her "friends."

Domica searched for Turtle's eyes in the dark to see if it was time. Was this it? But Turtle was looking at Stacey now, unmoving between them. She walked toward her, and they all counted to three, a brief but steady chant that seemed to come in a single voice.

A circle of feet thudded into Stacey's back and arms.

Thump, thump, thump.

Stacey was caught so unaware that her hands were slow to come up in defense. She loosed a gulp of air from her throat and went down all the way, a limp, unresisting rag doll in the grass. Then they were kicking her head.

Thump, thump.

"Stop!" she shouted now, finally finding the instinct to move her arms. But a belt appeared in Domica's hand, and she brought it down four times on Stacey's neck, the silver cutouts along one side glimmering in the airport lights.

Turtle chanted: "I . . . love . . . Tracy. Tracy . . . loves . . . me." And the refrain was delivered, and repeated, to the rhythm of her kicks.

They were in a fury now, steadily pounding her back and face. Stacey balled up, with her arms as a shell, but it was no use: They were at her from all sides.

"Why y'all doing this to me?" she cried out.

"Because you're a liar," came the answer from Turtle.

Stephanie ambled over from the picnic bench to plant a few kicks and went back to sit down again.

"I'm sorry, you guys. Pleeease!" Stacey said, her voice finally rising to a desperate pitch.

Dana didn't budge from her sweaty retreat in the back seat of the car. The remains of that pill left her immobile and spacey, and her body temperature soared. She was prone

now and couldn't see a thing. On the other hand, she heard
plenty. "I heard beating, muffled yells, loud talking," she
would say later. "It sounded like an unpadded football
game."

Minutes passed. Out came the pair of hugga-hugga orange
boxcutters. Tracy and Domica thumbed the blades out
through their plastic sheaths and then back in again, each
noisily strumming a row of tiny notches. Out and in. Out
and in.

It was a familiar sound from their afternoon at the little
black table at South Belmont, adjusting the very same blades
to the task of keeping ink inside a tattoo.

"Remember this?" Domica asked her. And because it
sounded so scary along with the *tick, tick, tick* of the blades,
the others said it too.

"Remember this?"

Stacey was silent, disbelieving. Until they began to slice
at her, with shallow, stinging cuts, and she cried out.

"My God, no!"

Domica caught her blade in Stacey's hair and *pfffft*, a
two-inch tuft fell into the grass. And another.

The blades were short but sharp. Turtle stepped into the
fray and felt Domica mistakenly slash the lower part of her
leg. She reached out and grabbed the knife from her—blade
first, because that's what was out there. Just as quickly,
Tracy grabbed it from Turtle, leaving behind a slice through
Turtle's palm. And then Tracy leaned over Stacey's back
and pulled the boxcutter across her spine.

Stacey screamed.

Several minutes more went by. The beating had slowed.
Stacey's blood would be staining the grass by now. Her
throat only allowed a whimper. Somehow she managed to
push the ground away and rise to her feet.

"C'mon, you guys, let's go." It was Stephanie, back at
the car now. She had had enough. Then she turned on the
headlights, and Dana, now upright, was able to see what
was going on for the first time.

"I saw Stacey standing up wearing a white t-shirt and her back was covered in blood." Dana would remember this quite clearly. "All three girls were standing around her. I saw Tracy push her down, and then I saw Domica go to the picnic table, pick up a cinder block and throw it on her."

The white, cube-shaped chunk, which amounted to about half of a full cinder block, hit Stacey in the face.

Stacey was a mess by now. And suddenly there were so many decisions for her tormentors to make. What came next? They left her in the grass and drove away, only to return a few minutes later. They couldn't leave her there, they just couldn't, not that anybody yet offered a reason why.

Stacey had crawled some distance and then collapsed again by the pickup; she looked up when she saw the Tempo's lights. A faceless army approached on foot.

"Can you do me a favor?" she begged them slowly, pitifully, from the dirt.

"What do you want?" Tracy was impatient.

"Can y'all just take me to a pay phone? So I can call my mama's? I just want to be taken to a phone."

"Well, we can't," Domica told her. She was impatient too, even tyrannical. Gotta get this show on the road. If we're going to put her in the car, let's do it.

They had to hold her up, feet dragging, most of the way back to the car, while she chanted feebly, "Please don't hurt me anymore. Please don't hurt me anymore."

Stacey's eye was swollen shut and she had blood running down her forehead. She may not have seen right away that they were heading toward the trunk. As the group cleared first the front door and then the back, she became confused.

"We can't let you get in the car," Domica explained. "You know we can't. We don't want your blood on the car. If you want to ride in the trunk then we'll give you a ride."

Oh, nooo. Stacey hadn't even thought of that. No way. "I can't stay in tight places. I can't—"

"Well, it's that or nothing," said Domica.

"Please, just let me ride in the car and just lean on you in the car," she begged. "I won't be able to breathe for sure. I won't be able to breathe!"

They were at the trunk now. A small, woolen Winnie-the-Pooh blanket was yanked aside and removed to the back seat, where Dana clutched it thankfully.

"Get the fuck in," Turtle told Stacey at the trunk.

"Pick her up and put her in there," said Domica.

And so they did. Stacey half-stepped, half-fell, inside, winding quickly into a fetal position with her head at the right side of the trunk. Domica slammed it shut, and they drove off.

The metal-on-metal sound of that trunk coming down must have been louder than Stacey's screams out in the field or the taunts of her attackers. Because it wasn't until the Tempo had cleared the driveway and made it back out onto Nash Road that Denny Harrison finally opened the back door of the warehouse. Something had interrupted his sleep.

A quick look around revealed nothing. It wasn't light enough to see that there was blood on his truck, not that he had any reason to check. And so he went back to his couch.

The dark, airless horror inside Stephanie's trunk flushed adrenaline into Stacey's weary limbs. They were barely out of Marsh Field when she started banging. And yelling. Stephanie pulled the car onto the shoulder of Cogbill Road and popped the trunk. Domica went to see about shutting her up.

"You have to be quiet."

"I need a phone. *Can't* you take me to a hospital?" Her voice was a whine now.

"No." *Slam.*

And so it was back to the same question: Where to take her and what to do?

The options became fewer and fewer as the skewed logic of fear began to catch on inside the car. More than one good conscience cried out: Take her to a hospital! But every time somebody put that into words it sounded wrong, seemed impossible. Before, Stacey was an irritant; now she had the power to destroy them all.

"We gotta get rid of her," Tracy said. She was sweating hard. "She's gonna rat us out. We're gonna go to jail."

"Yeah," chimed Stephanie. "I mean, why should she be trusted now?"

"Her tongue needs to be cut out," said Tracy.

It was a horrible thing to say but it made sense. It wasn't enough, really.

"She's still gonna know how to write, you know," said Dana.

"Her fingers need to be cut off," suggested Domica.

Stacey was banging again. Shit, somebody was going to hear her. There were no driveways at all, and no shoulder, but not a single other car on the road either. And so Stephanie just braked. This time, everyone but Dana got out. Left to right, it was Stephanie, Domica, Tracy, and Turtle.

"Take me to a hospital," Stacey begged them from the cave where she had been trapped for half an hour by now. She whimpered, shivered, a vision of frailty in the dim trunk light. Looking up at these somehow unfamiliar faces lined up and staring down as if into an open casket, she spoke again.

"I swear I won't say anything. I won't mention anybody's names. I'll go back to Lynchburg. I'll never see you guys again. You know, I . . . I'll be even."

But it was too late for that. Any earlier moments of pity, stray words about leaving Stacey at some emergency room door, were forgotten now. Stephanie reached down with one of the boxcutters and gashed her from hip to knee. The others spat. And Domica relieved her of that watch.

"Give me your rings," Domica now told her.

"Give 'em to her," instructed Tracy.

Stacey began to oblige, slowly, painfully. But then she stopped, looked up.

"You can have them all except this one."

Stacey had lots of rings but there was one she never took off: an antique-style band with a garnet that had belonged to Michelle, her roommate in Lynchburg. This must have felt like her last connection to life right then. She screamed as it was taken from her.

"Please don't hurt me anymore!"

Now Stacey was sobbing again, choking on her own words as the trunk fell.

14:

All the turnoffs were looking the same now. Stephanie was driving in circles. Nothing was dark and deserted enough. A dirt road would lead into some trees and there would be cars or a house. Near Pocahontas State Park, on a dense, woodsy stretch of Nash Road, they glimpsed a pipe gate blocking a logging road on their left, but sped by too quickly to make the entrance.

Stephanie turned the car around up near the rough beginnings of a housing development that was going to be called The Highlands and then onto the little road they had spied. The Tempo came to a stop at the rail, and before Stephanie cut the lights they could see that the clearing was long, straight, and protected by a canopy of soaring pines.

Stacey was plucked from the trunk, crumpled and weaker now. "Please don't hurt me," she whined.

She teetered around the car, leaning on her captors, and when she saw the gate and the blackness behind it she began to cry. Stephanie was standing by the driver's side door, and it was open, the car's alarm system beeping insistently.

Then for a few moments out in front of the car, it was back to the one-on-one where it had all started. "Turtle . . ." Stacey took in a sharp gulp of air and released another sob. "Why are you doing this to me?" she asked.

"You lied to me," Turtle told her. And still, blood running from Stacey's body, and murder just a few thoughts away for the circle of girls around her, this was somehow an answer to that question. And this: "I love Tracy."

Stacey's reply was trapped in that same surreal spiral—the logic of a battered spirit, to be sure.

"But I love you," she said.

Turtle hit her then, and told her again, "I love Tracy."

Everybody but Dana was there at the gate now. Stacey was sturdy enough on her feet to get around it on her own, along with the others. But then Stephanie made a long, vertical slice down her back, and she fell onto the road in a crunch of gravel, dirt, and pine needles.

Okay, was the feeling, go ahead and cut her; nobody was seeing Stacey's pain anymore. But still, the plan was to march, and so they needed her back on her feet. If the thought persisted in everyone's minds that they were just leaving her here, just delaying her escape to a phone or to other people, well then walking a little ways into the woods still fit that scenario.

"I can't walk."

"Well fine, then," Domica told her. "We'll drag you."

"No, let me help," she protested.

And so they hoisted her as a group and propped her between them, with Tracy on her left, Domica behind, and Turtle off on the right.

Stephanie gave Tracy the blade she had just wielded and returned carefully, painfully, to the car. She was definitely not up for this kind of walk and everybody knew it.

Dana was quiet but alert when Stephanie arrived.

"Are they really going to kill her?" she asked.

"I don't know."

Stacey herself seemed to have thought so by then.

"Don't kill me," she begged as the trio moved her slowly up into the dark, the earth under their feet getting wetter as they walked. "*Please* let me call my mom."

No one was hitting her just then, or stabbing her, or throwing anything at her. Rather, she was pressed up against the bodies of her attackers—Tracy in particular, who had her right arm around Stacey's shoulders. The burden of holding Stacey off the ground made their muscles taut, and she must have felt their power over her in a new, direct way. But what began to clarify the purpose of this procession—for all of them—was the direction and distance they were walking, farther and farther away from other people, from safety, from options.

Perhaps it was this thought that energized Stacey now and filled her lungs with a surprising gust of air.

"God, y'all! Leave me alone!" she screamed. "Leave me alone!"

It was much too loud. They couldn't have her making so much noise. Tracy clamped her hand over Stacey's mouth.

Pretty soon they had put a long distance behind them, and so they stopped, at a low, muddy place in the road. They were something like 450 feet from the car by now, and there was still no sign of houses or cars or lights of any kind.

The next several minutes went quickly, but also calmly at first. They seemed to know now that they weren't leaving her this way, that something horrible was about to happen—and that deliberation might help put it off or see that it was done right. They started by taking off her clothes. Tracy lifted the "We Hate Her" t-shirt over Stacey's head and Domica slid off the blue Champion basketball shorts with the white waistband folded over.

By now the shirt was not just stained with blood but cut right through in places, especially down the middle of the back.

They complained aloud about the mud underfoot, and on their shoes. And then it occurred to them without anybody saying so that they might suffocate her in it. They knocked her off her feet and pushed her face into the road. She struggled, and they held down the back of her head. But then she managed to turn again and face them, and she lashed out, smacking Turtle in the neck.

Turtle now grabbed her hand. And Tracy asked Stacey a strange question.

"You're not gonna say anything to anybody, are you?"

"No," she gasped. "No."

As if there was an out here, as if she were going to have a chance to say anything to anybody not present here and now on this logging road. In retrospect, it was more like an announcement of the reason *why* she was going to have to die—the ceremonial crossing of a line.

If something more needed to be said by way of a vote, it never happened. But in the frenzy of flying mud and flesh-on-flesh pounding that followed, these brazen, confused girls were suddenly trying to kill Stacey.

They were also learning, in the very first minutes of this effort, that killing somebody without a deadly weapon is a very hard thing to do. They felt stumped, outsmarted by their task. They yelled, "Why won't you die?" as if to give her some part in this, as if it were a battle instead of a slaughter.

Now they were kicking her, which made Stacey curl up again. She continued to cry out and her assailants chanted, "Shut up. Shut up!" Then Tracy dropped to her knees and straddled her, glumly, deliberately, setting about the task of stuffing mud into her mouth. Turtle got down behind her, on Stacey's legs.

Tracy put Stacey in a headlock, trying to break her neck.

"Her neck won't break," she muttered, worked-up and panting.

She had one hand around the back of Stacey's neck, with her head cradled out in front of her. Now she reached into her pocket, put the boxcutter on Stacey's throat, pulled it across, and released her head again with a quiet *plunk* into the mud.

There was a scramble, and nobody could see quite what was happening. But then Domica was down there and taking the cutter from Tracy's hand and jabbing its shallow blade into Stacey's chest, over and over. Her hand became a machine, beating out a steady rhythm against the ribs above Stacey's heart.

Tracy was still straddling her in the mud, and she had Stacey's right arm trapped, but for a moment the left one was up and swinging at Domica, trying to push her away, trying to block the pumping motion, to keep the blade from coming down again. Turtle grabbed that left arm, held it down, and Stacey was pinned.

Domica demanded, "Give me your heart, bitch."

When she finally stopped, exhausted and breathing hard, she got to her feet and flung the blade to the ground. But then she thought better of that: She switched on her lighter and found it again in the mud.

It was right about this time that Stephanie flashed the lights of the car. She had heard the screams and seen the flicker of the lighter, and waited so long that she couldn't just sit still anymore and do nothing.

Domica and Tracy seemed to feel it too: It was enough, time to go. They pulled away from the puddle and started walking back down the road—Tracy in bare feet, having left her sandals behind, buried in the mud along with one of the boxcutter handles.

The headlights of the car fully illuminated the logging road now, all the way down to where Turtle was kneeling. In the glow she could see right into Stacey's eyes when she turned her head and looked up at her.

Cindy Cull was awakened before dawn by a noise under her bedroom window.

"Stephanie?"

"I'm just here to go to the bathroom," came Stephanie's voice. "I'm going to Turtle's."

"Okay. Lock the door."

"Okay."

Otherwise, there was no talking. Green Leigh in the first hours of the morning rested under a fragile kind of quiet. Voices carried easily over the concrete parking rectangles adjacent to each trailer, down through the low, sparse trees and up against all the metal siding. Dottie Drive was in the back, well away from any stray nighttime traffic, and as quiet as Maria, Sula, George, Vicky, or any of the other tiny streets crisscrossing the trailer park.

Stephanie knew about keeping the noise down at night, from growing up in such close proximity to hundreds of other people—and from the complaints that had poured in to her mom after the debauched acid nights of the week before.

Stephanie was in the house for maybe two minutes, just long enough to leave a note for a friend coming by the next day: She was going to be late because Dana needed a ride to work at noon. Stephanie would be back here at the trailer as quickly as she could.

She pulled a Coke out of the fridge and went back outside to the car.

"My mom's up," she whispered to the others, climbing back in behind the wheel.

The drive to South Belmont Avenue was timed to the rising of the sun. Going north on the Interstate, normally a frenetic jostle, it seemed they were entirely alone in the world. They sat in silence while the first light of Sunday began to brighten the inside of the car. It was all there with them: the single remaining boxcutter, their muddy clothes, even the bloody scraps they'd pulled from Stacey's body.

The adrenaline finally began to drain from their bodies, and in its place came headaches and cigarette breath and a great, alcohol-induced thirst.

"What the fuck happened to her?" Turtle asked.

Now they were strategizing. This was a question somebody would be asking of them, surely, sometime very soon.

"We dropped her off," posited Tracy.

"We kicked her out of the car," Turtle added.

Somebody suggested that maybe the two irrepressible lovers had been smooching and Stacey had gotten jealous. It was a great idea.

"Yeah, me and Tracy were making out," Turtle said, picking up that thought and seeing how it sounded. "She got pissed off, we let her out of the car, near Byrd Park, and that's your story. We're fucking sticking to that."

They sat with this lie for a minute, digesting it, running it through their panicked, tired minds, and it seemed like it would work. Especially when Domica raised the stakes for them just as the Tempo was finally crossing the James River.

"Y'all *better* stick to it," she said. "If any of y'all talks, the same thing could happen to them."

By the time they left the expressway, it had become clear that dumping the weapons and even their clothes would be a really good idea. The pull to get home overwhelmed them, though, and so it wasn't until they neared South Belmont Avenue that there was a plan of any sort.

One house over from number 210, there's a dusty little alleyway that skirts kitchen doors and back yards for several blocks, as small streets just like it do all over Richmond. Tall green Dumpsters with sturdy black tops line it, left and right.

Stephanie drove down a ways and stopped the Tempo right alongside one of these so that Turtle could reach it through the window. She leaned out, nudged open the top, and let loose a single orange plastic handle and miscellaneous pieces of blade.

Robyn was still awake behind the closed door of her bedroom when she heard the slow, weary racket of their return sometime after 4:30. The hour wasn't alarming, and she probably wouldn't have known they were one person short even if she'd been listening for clues. In fact, it may have been the familiar sound of having a crowd in the house that sent her to sleep.

Turtle and Tracy went straight out to the back porch, where they stripped down to nothing and left behind the clothes that seemed the most badly stained by their victim's blood, which was basically everything that Tracy and Stacey had had on, plus Domica's sneakers. Turtle also left her hat—Tracy's hat. They'd have to get rid of that stuff tomorrow. Turtle put her crusty wet Airwalk sneakers inside the front door so that they wouldn't go along by mistake.

Domica disappeared around the corner and Dana collapsed upstairs on Turtle's bed. Stephanie was glad to have pocketed one of Dana's sleeping pills for herself, and now she swallowed it hopefully, and stretched out on the sofa-bed.

In the shower, Turtle and Tracy rubbed at each other's skin and watched a trail of mud and blood—mostly fresh from Turtle's own veins now—disappear down the drain. Tracy squeezed Turtle's hand with both of her own, but the bleeding wouldn't stop. Her leg was a mess too. And she was in a panic.

"It's gonna be okay," Tracy told her.

"Yeah, okay."

They put on fresh clothes in Turtle's room and headed down to the couch in the living room. Domica was back now in a clean pair of sweat pants and already sleeping next to Stephanie.

"Come here," Tracy told Turtle. "Let's try to get some sleep."

PART FIVE

Rats

"She knew she didn't want to tell us everything 'cause she didn't want us to think she was some sort of monster."

—Karla

15:

Early Sunday mornings in summer, Cary Street is all pear trees and empty parking spots. The espresso drinkers are up, hanging over weekend sections of *The Washington Post* on the patio at Betsy's Coffeehouse, but they arrive on foot and their conversations are hushed and short.

Without the usual clamor of shoppers, you get a better sense of Carytown the living neighborhood. You notice the sudden shabbiness along its southern edge, for instance, a narrow section of mostly wooden houses bordered on the other side by the I95 expressway, so near and yet so far from Betsy's mochaccinos.

A block down from the coffeehouse and another two over, in the dappled yard of the red-brick, U-shaped Old Dominion home for the aged, a grizzled man in a wheelchair studies something small in the grass. A pair of nurses in white shoes cross a drooping porch and trek habitually up South Belmont Avenue toward the bus.

Number 210 faces east, toward Old Dominion—and the morning sun. The top half of the house gets it straight-on, and it creeps inside between Levolors. Downstairs, the porch roof shields the front door and an overgrown bush covers what the broken blind in the lone front window might otherwise expose.

"What'd' y'all do with Stacey?"

Robyn barked this into a houseful of slumbering bodies. She kicked the couch, where Tracy and Turtle slept entwined. But there was not a stir, not a flickering eyelid.

Stephanie and Domica were just as still as stone on the pullout bed in the dining room.

Not that Robyn was expecting an answer. It was more of a parting shot than an inquiry—a dig at the hangovers and a routine announcement that she was off to work, out of the house. A friend was going to drive her. No problem, don't get up. Here I go being the grownup.

It was a good question, though, with no sign of the besieged roommate. Almost as good as the next one she asked:

"What? 'D y'all kill Stacey?"

Now Tracy opened her eyes and looked at Robyn. She blinked and announced, "Look, I have to take a shit," getting herself quickly to the stairs.

Next, Domica was up and in a hurry. "Fuck. I gotta get outta here. What time is it?" She rubbed her head and considered her parched mouth and the night before in the same horrible instant. The ordinariness of her Sunday chores was cool and forgiving. The front door let in patchy sunlight and Robyn headed out behind her into the day.

Upstairs, Tracy's brain pondered the muddy evidence on the back porch. They had to get rid of that stuff, but where? She pictured Sandy's place, and the faithful army of garbage Dumpsters scattered among the parking circles. Matchpoint seemed so far away, so absolutely separate from the world of Turtle—and Stacey; the world that was maybe about to cave in on her. Mostly, what Matchpoint must have seemed, right then, was safe.

Pretty soon Tracy was wrestling a wet, crusty wad of t-shirts, shoes, underwear, and shorts into a paper Ukrop's grocery bag and a plastic one with black-and-white stripes and "Footlocker" printed across the front in blue and red. She tiptoed across the dining room floor and delicately fished car keys from Stephanie's purse—her own car was still at Sandy's. The chunky brown cakes that had once been Turtle's Airwalk sneakers would stay where she had left them at the front door.

* * *

Turtle was finally upright when Tracy got back from Match-point and she collapsed beside her on the slippery green sleeping bag that passed for a slipcover. It was hot out there, several degrees warmer than Saturday, and Tracy was damp from it.

She leaned in to take a closer look at Turtle's leg, still bloody this morning.

"We have to fucking clean that out. It's so deep, Turtle."

"It hurts bad."

The cut in her hand was raw too.

"I'm so sorry, I didn't mean to cut you," Tracy told her.

"It's okay," Turtle said.

Focusing on the wounds, and Tracy's apology, was easier than trying to talk about their night, their future, their feel-ings—and any bigger apology that anyone might owe. But their minds raced with unspoken questions and a suffocating mix of love and fear. Turtle wondered, What happens now? Do I trust her?

"Everything's gonna be all right," Tracy cooed. She touched Turtle's face and kissed her.

Yet Tracy was wary too. Turtle said later that she needed to discuss a very important lingering matter about what had happened in the dark on that logging road, and Tracy was a little surprised when she claimed that she had made up the part about goring Stacey with a stick at the end there. Was Turtle trying to get away with something?

"Do you think she's, um, dead or what?" Tracy asked.

"I don't know. When I left her, she wasn't. Tracy, what'd you do with all her clothes?"

"I put 'em in the Dumpster over at Sandy's house. You a'ight?"

"Yeah. I'm fine."

"Cool. Cause I'm a'ight too."

Turtle and Tracy also talked about running away to Cal-ifornia, but only as if it were one of a range of options. And they danced around the idea of sharing their secret with somebody else. The unspoken promise between them: I won't tell anybody, don't worry. The real deal, building on months of mistrust: I'm going to tell, and I know you will too.

"Joe, man, wake up. I'm freakin' out. Joe, man, this is fucked up."

"Hmmm?"

When Dana opened her eyes, at about eleven o'clock, she was on Turtle's bed—coughing blood. Never mind work. She'd call in sick to the Bagel Bakery. But right now Turtle was whispering in her ear.

"I need to tell somebody," Turtle went on. She seemed about to burst.

Then Tracy was there and displaying a row of raw knuckles for Dana's consideration. "Check it out," she said, and you could see that Stacey's braces had stripped the skin away—when Tracy was pushing mud between her lips a short seven or so hours before.

Stephanie, finally awakened from her narcotic slumber by a phone call from Claire, went home about 12:30, as soon as she learned that Dana wasn't going to be needing a ride to work after all. The others watched television and made a few phone calls.

And then some more: Tracy left a total of about 15 messages on Sandy's phone machine that day, ten of them crammed into the earlier hours.

"Hey, what's going on?" Tracy was light and friendly at first, and it had obviously slipped her mind that Sandy was spending the day with her ex-girlfriend. "Just seein' what you're doin'."

Tracy and Turtle were singing on the second message, and there was loud music on the third. On the fourth, they were telling jokes. There were other people in the background.

In the early afternoon, Tracy's voice began to get serious. "Hey, just wanted to see what you were doing." Then, "I really wanna talk to you. Give me a call." And finally, "Hey, where the fuck are you? Call me."

*   *   *

What a pleasure to find Karla at home and answering the phone with the perky "Hel-*lo*?" that still fluttered Tracy's heart. Karla made a big fuss. She had been thinking about Tracy a lot, hoping for another invitation to South Belmont Avenue, and feeling much less worried about her boyfriend's disapproval. He didn't have to know *everything*.

So could the twins come over? Please? Karla was supposed to see a movie at the old Byrd Theatre that night, right there on Cary Street, and Danielle had tickets to Lynyrd Skynyrd. They'd stop by first. In the afternoon, around four.

"We're all going to California," Tracy happened to mention before hanging up.

Sunday's first visitors to 210 South Belmont came unannounced, though. Not that there was anything strange about that. Peter and Will, several giggly days into their courtship by now, knocked at around three. The idea was to check on Stacey, and the boys were confused by the strange moods and unexplained activities of the afternoon.

Turtle and Tracy, wrapped in each other's limbs on the pullout couch, were distracted but cheery. Peter and Will noticed that Turtle had a huge gash on her leg. "I was rollerblading," she told them, "and I fuckin' fell down."

Next came a veiled version of the truth.

"Where's Stacey?" Peter asked.

"I beat the shit out of her last night and I haven't seen her since," Turtle said.

Okay, either that was a joke or it was like Friday's boxing session—survivable. Peter would find out for himself from Stacey, if not today, then Monday; they were on the same shift at the Annabel Lee. As for Will, he was too distracted by Tracy to pay Turtle's toughie routine much mind. Tracy was so charming, so *silly*.

"She'd fall down a couple times and then get back up and laugh. She was just so happy. Like a little puppy. I remember thinking, She and Turtle are so different. Because

Turtle is so, like, rough on the exterior and so 'I'm gonna kick your ass.' And, you know, here's Tracy, bouncing around and having a good time. And talking to everybody."

Then the twins drove up. And Domica came by to get her shoes.

"Are you okay?" Turtle asked Domica.

"I'm fine," she answered, but here was another odd moment, as far as the guests were concerned. It sounded more like, "I *guess* I'm okay—considering." Considering what? Karla wanted to know.

With Tracy entertaining the twins and charming the boys, Turtle found a few rare minutes of privacy upstairs and reached Diane. She had been there for Turtle in her darkest days as a child mom, an unhappy little girl on her own; surely her second mother would help her now.

"Diane, I need to talk to you about something," she told her. "I need to come to your house. It's very important."

Turtle made a theatrical re-entry downstairs and concocted an emergency. "I've gotta go *right now*," she announced. "My baby's sick." With her hair flying around and her eye blacked and all those boxcutter wounds, you had to believe something was wrong.

The boys gave Turtle a ride over to Diane's West End place and quickly figured that the kid wasn't sick, not with Turtle laughing and singing along with the car radio like that. Then Marisa wasn't even *at* Diane's.

The charade didn't work for Tracy either—and she was the one Turtle was hoping to fool. Tracy figured Turtle was a free agent now—and about to spill the beans. In which case, she would do the same.

"I've got a secret, and I'm going to tell you," Tracy said, looking down at the twins from the top of a stool that Robyn had constructed from a seat cushion and an old planter. They sat in the dining room, Karla on the sofabed and Danielle in a chair. Tracy was girlish, even perky. But there was something very grownup about the look in her eyes. This couldn't be good.

"You gotta promise me you won't—"

"What? Tell us!"

"We're your best friends! Tell us."

And so she did.

"Um, we killed Stacey."

Tracy's words were ridiculous, so the pause that followed seemed out of place too.

"What are you talking about?" Karla was not believing this.

"We killed her," Tracy repeated.

"Oh my God! You're lying. No way. That's bullshit, Tracy!"

Then Tracy told them what had happened, from Stacey's first unaware moments at Marsh Field, all the way through to Tracy's late morning drive to get rid of those bags. She left out very little, but sometimes you could see her heading toward a horrifying detail—and steering right by. The twins were a chorus of "Oh no!"'s and "Tracy!"'s, verging on the parental.

"Only God can take lives," Danielle told Tracy at one point, devastating her.

When Tracy started to cry, Karla was standing there next to her. She kissed Tracy's hands—and stopped to look at them when her lips touched torn, ragged skin. "Oh my God, oh my *God*! What happened to your knuckles?"

Tracy needed to get her stuff at Sandy's, she said finally. Her car, her clothes. Things she'd need to take with her on the road, on this surreal California escape that the twins eventually stopped asking her about.

On the way to Matchpoint, Tracy brightened a little. She told Karla that she looked beautiful, and put her head out the window and screamed. Karla told her to shut up, that she was embarrassing her. And when they said goodbye, Karla watched her cross the patch of grass outside Sandy's door and thought: This might be the last time I see her free again.

*   *   *

"Okay, I got a phone call. They found her. She's in the hospital."

Tracy was at the pay phone outside Sandy's empty apartment, without a key. She was finding it very hard to think straight while trapped in the delicate landscape of potted, blooming trees and tiny, numbered awnings. But surely this tale of hers would keep Turtle from telling Diane about last night. If she already had, it would stop Diane from calling the police.

"Don't worry," Tracy told Turtle. "She's in, like, intensive care. She's in critical condition, but she's gonna be all right. I don't think she's said anything."

The news took Turtle entirely by surprise. She'd given some thought to the concept of murder, figuring without focusing on it too much that after all these hours, Stacey was dead. Now she scrambled to make sense of this new idea.

But mostly, in that very moment, she was happy about appeasing Diane, who had hunkered down with her girlfriend to the task of bandaging Turtle's leg but had pretty much drawn the sympathy line there. In plain fact, she was furious. Turtle had spent the afternoon in tears.

"Diane, it's all good," Turtle now told her. "She's in the hospital. She's all right, she's not dead. And I don't think she's gonna tell on me. She'll tell on them, but she's not gonna tell on me."

The problem, as Turtle saw it, was that things were moving a lot more quickly now. The vast expanse of Sunday had trickled away in the numbing exercise of waiting. Now they could only react. It was time to get serious, time to make a plan, get their stories straight.

16:

At about one o'clock, Stephanie put thirty-five cents into the motel phone up the street from Green Leigh; her mom's phone was out. "I need to talk to you," she told Claire over the hum of traffic on Jefferson Davis Highway. "It's really important."

Not right now, though, because her friend Cherie was coming over to the trailer. Stephanie would come by Claire's later, at four or five. Claire told her that was okay and hung up the phone.

But now Claire's imagination was running wild: Stephanie had done something horrible with those girls, she guessed, something violent. "For some reason, the way she said it, that thought had actually gone through my mind," Claire would say later. "Not exactly that. Not specifically about Stacey. But I kinda tried to put it out of mind till I could see her."

Stephanie endured her visit from Cherie in virtual silence. Cindy fixed spaghetti for lunch and the friends watched television in Stephanie's room. The noise in Stephanie's head— *I gotta talk to Claire, I gotta talk to Claire*—was unbearable, but it didn't show. Cindy, struggling to get the trailer back in shape after the recklessness of her time away, didn't get a hint that anything was wrong. Sulking was normal for Stephanie.

At about five, Stephanie drove her mom's car up to Claire's parents' house—the Tempo was too much of a mess—and limped, stoney-faced, into her bedroom. It was some time before she could lose the studied flatness of her afternoon. She fidgeted on the bed and recited the events of the night before like a story she had heard from somebody else.

All of it was new to Claire, cut off for so long from Stephanie's other life. "When she came over," Claire would remember, "she started to unfold how they discussed how Stacey had been lying to them about relationships going on in the house. And how they were going to beat her up and make her leave town."

Tears came soon enough, and Stephanie's body began to shake. Claire held her at first; poor thing, she'd been through so much. But then the story was out, and Claire realized that she had no comfort to spare. Those miserable months of Stephanie's indifference came back to her. Did her vain, superficial pursuit of these girls have no end? Was there anything worse that Stephanie could have done than help kill someone?

"How could you be part of that?" Claire needed to know. "How could you go along with it? Why didn't you do anything?"

Stephanie was quiet now, except for the sobs. And she was no longer looking at Claire. She wiped her glasses on her shirt. The questions mounted: "Do you realize what you've done? How can you sit there like that?"

It seemed like she would never stop crying. "I don't know what to do. I'm so scared. I don't know what happened."

The ringing phone was a horrible reminder that time was passing quickly in the real world. Even worse, it was Turtle.

"No." Stephanie wouldn't talk to her. "No."

Claire insisted, holding the receiver up to Stephanie's fuzzy head.

Turtle wanted everybody to run away with her to California. She wanted Stephanie to go get her car and drive up there to Carytown and take them all away. Claire took her usual dissenting role, but this time it was with the righteousness of a patient wife who has now had enough.

"You're going to get caught!" she announced when Stephanie was off again. "Don't even think that they're not going to find you. You left a huge trail of evidence.''

It was too much for Stephanie. She was paralyzed. And crushed by Claire's message—that she was stupid and powerless and that it was too late to run.

''Stephanie,'' she said, ''you've got to turn yourself in.''

Then Turtle was on the phone again, coming at Stephanie even harder the second time around. ''You know,'' she told her, ''we can get away if we run now. We'll get away. We have enough hours before they find out.''

And then, ''You can't tell anybody, Stephanie. You know what'll happen if you tell anybody. They won't believe you. You'll go down just as much as we will.''

17:

It was after seven when Sandy's pickup sailed through the front gates at Matchpoint, down the sloping asphalt drive, past the tennis courts and the swimming pool, and into a painted slot outside her home. Tracy was sitting by a Dumpster. She said she had been waiting a long time. When they wrapped their arms around each other, Sandy noticed that Tracy's clothes were soaked through with sweat.

"Hey, I missed you today," Sandy told her.

"Yeah, me too."

The familiar beige wall-to-wall carpeting in Sandy's tiny, curtained living room seemed to draw Tracy down. She stretched out on her back and pulled Sandy on top.

"Hey, what did you do today?" Sandy wanted to know.

Tracy paused. Let her listen to the phone machine first, she figured, so she knows I tried to call her, so she remembers that she loves me.

"You got so many messages on your machine."

"Really?"

"Yeah, they're all from me."

"Well, let me go check."

It took several minutes to run the tape. Sandy listened on her feet, grimaced to hear Turtle's voice and all the laughing, and then noticed Tracy's mood crash at some point later in the day. As far as Sandy could tell, though, all that frantic calling was about Tracy missing her, and she felt a mixture of warmth at being loved so much and bemusement about the teenybopper behavior.

"So, what *did* you do today?" Sandy asked, returning to the warm stretch of Tracy's stomach.

"Sandy, I really . . . I gotta talk to you. I gotta tell you something."

"What, honey?" Now Sandy was teasing her with little kisses, not really wanting to talk at all. "Can we do this later?" she asked.

"No, I really need to talk to you. I need to tell you something. I did something really bad."

Sandy could put the kissing on hold, no problem, but she was still not ready to be serious. She got up for a glass of water. "Okay, whadya do? Kill somebody or rob a bank?"

"Well, I didn't rob a bank" came the answer from the living room floor.

It probably took a matter of seconds for Sandy to respond, but it felt like longer. Tracy's words hung in the air like a vaguely sour but undefinable smell.

"What do you mean?" Sandy asked when she was back in the living room, and pressing herself into Tracy again.

"I think we killed Stacey."

Sandy rolled onto the carpet. She was awake now.

"What do you mean *you think*? What are you talking about, Tracy?"

"We killed Stacey."

Sandy looked into Tracy's eyes, hoping for a joke or an easy explanation. But her face was more like a mirror, studying Sandy right back. Still, Sandy couldn't quite hear the news.

"How do you know she's dead?"

"I *know* she's dead. I *know* we killed her."

Sandy took hold of Tracy's hand just then and led her into the bedroom. It seemed to beckon like a last, soft comfort—or maybe an arbiter of reality. "Come here," she said. They stretched out next to each other.

"Tracy, tell me what's going on."

Once again, she described Marsh Field, the kicking, the cutting, the driving around in a frenzy with Stacey in the trunk. And once again, she cried. Every word let loose a tiny wave of relief, and then pure pain.

Meanwhile, Sandy's own feelings were beginning to sort

themselves out: She was repulsed. "It just kinda blew me away, and I didn't touch her," Sandy would remember. "I just kinda rolled away from her and listened."

"Tracy, you need to call 911," she said finally.

"But she's dead."

"Maybe not, maybe she's still alive. There's a chance she's still there, breathing or something. Tracy, *call*."

"I'm going to Mexico."

"Tracy, don't run. Just stick around. Go to your grand-mother's or something. Just wait and see what the hell's going on."

Now it occurred to Sandy that she was afraid too.

"Just don't call from my house," she sputtered. "Good God, those people will trace it back and come to me and pull me into this. Go to a pay phone and call 911 and ex-plain where this happened and go check it out."

Turtle called at about 9. Sandy couldn't hear exactly what she said, but she didn't like it. She was already blaming Turtle for this nightmare. It seemed like the only way not to hate Tracy.

"Don't ever let that bitch call my house again," Sandy told her when she hung up. "She fucking got you into this."

But now Tracy was crying harder. And Sandy realized that she couldn't bear to touch her. She looked at her lover's hands and noticed they were still muddy. There was dirt under her fingernails. Tracy watched her eyes.

"Don't hate me. Don't hate me!" Tracy begged.

"Tracy, I don't hate you. I just think you better go, and do what you gotta do. Just don't run."

Moments later, they were at the front door. "Well aren'tcha gonna give me a hug or a kiss or something?" Tracy wondered. Sandy reached up mechanically. She told her she loved her and said, "I'll talk to you later."

18:

It was after nine now, and the sun had set. Turtle was still frantically summoning the troops, dialing and redialing from the cordless phone in her bedroom. And then she looked up and Tracy was standing in the doorway, her beaded choker peeking over the top of a white t-shirt. Turtle had forgotten that she had so little hair now.

"Are you all right?" Tracy asked.

"Yeah." Turtle's green eyes were ablaze. "Stephanie should be here in a little while. We've gotta talk about this. I haven't fucking found Mica, she won't answer her phone. I'm gonna have to walk around there."

"All right," Tracy said. "I'm gonna go make some Oodles of Noodles."

A friend arrived with some pot. Tracy got a little high and went poking around in the kitchen for a package of Ramen.

As Turtle was coming downstairs, there was a knock at the door—a serious kind of knock. She looked to her left and there was Tracy, frozen in her tracks, staring back. And Dana, doing the same.

"Oh shit," said Turtle.

19:

Wayne Felice was always very close to his daughters. They told him everything; not even the details of their teenage love lives were off limits. It was all Karla could do, after dropping Tracy off at Sandy's, not to stop along the road back to Chesterfield and unload this horrible new burden from a pay phone. Danielle had gone to the Lynyrd Skynyrd show; Karla headed home to the house across the street from Meadowbrook High. Thank God, he was there.

"Dad, I've gotta talk to you," she told him. It was traditional that they go outside for private conversations; Wayne let the back door slam shut behind them and looked down at his daughter.

"Dad, this is what happened. She killed this girl," Karla told him. Describing the rest was one of the hardest things she had ever had to do.

Karla was always a little shocked by her father's reactions to things—usually because he was perceptive so far beyond her own abilities. But this time he really blew her away.

"It doesn't surprise me," he told her.

"What?"

"I've always thought something like this was going to happen. She was a timebomb waiting to go off."

Karla was quiet for a minute. Back in the hot seat, between her family and the onetime love of her life, for once there was nothing further to add. And then her father said something truly scary.

"We've gotta call the police."

"No. Dad, I swore to her. I can't—I can't do that."

"What about that girl out in the woods, all by herself, wanting her mother? Tracy already lost her rights. She killed someone, and that's over the line. We loved her, but I'm calling the police."

The uniformed cop who answered Wayne's call patiently took down some notes. Karla hoped her story was as far-fetched as the guy's casual demeanor seemed to suggest. Instead, she spent the night driving around Chesterfield County and the city of Richmond in a squad car.

At the East Coast convenience store on Route 10, she answered questions into a tape recorder about what Tracy had told her. Some detectives headed off to check out Marsh Field, and another drove Karla north.

At Matchpoint, she watched cops poke around in some Dumpsters—and saw Sandy leave her apartment and drive away. Inside the car where she waited, the radio crackled with something about South Belmont Avenue, and it sounded like they weren't just talking about it, they were there.

20:

Walter Marsh was chopping wood on his land late Sunday when the cops pulled up. They wanted to know when he had been there last and whether anybody in the area had mentioned anything strange from the night before. And then when they'd scoped out the place, they picked up part of a .blood-stained cinder block. They also found two large rings and some cuttings of brown human hair—all in a six-foot radius of bloody grass.

Denny Harrison and his white pickup truck, also bloodied, were long gone by then.

21:

"The term that we use is a defensive position. They close up on you. They'll cross their arms or legs. I could actually see her arms trembling, you know? That's when she knew that I knew, and we both knew. That's when it hit me like a ton of bricks that hey, they really did do this."

—Detective Dave Zeheb

Detective Dave Zeheb is a clean-cut, serious man. He wears his near-black, thinning hair cropped close, and his neck is shaved carefully above the crisply ironed collars of his shirts. He chuckles softly about the way readers of *Moby Dick* get his Lebanese name wrong. But as a cop he's Joe Friday—deadpan, bolt-upright by nature, and quite sure about liking his job.

"You guys get paid for this?" he marveled back in 1987 when he followed some Chesterfield County officers around as a volunteer, a Ukrop's grocery store employee looking for a career move. He aced the 24-week training and had no trouble making detective and getting assigned to the prestigious Crimes Against Persons Unit.

Weekends in the summer of 1997, Detective Zeheb and his partner, Rick Mormando, were rotating shifts: One would do daytime duty with the other taking over in the late afternoon. On Sunday, July 27th, Detective Zeheb finished up at about 4:30 and headed home to his wife and six-year-old daughter.

It was about a quarter to nine when the phone rang. De-

tective Zeheb was deep into a really good episode of
"Touched by an Angel." But something was going on—
Rick would need some help. A young lady was missing
since the night before. They had an address where she was
supposed to be staying up in the city, in Carytown. Maybe
Dave could check it out.

Detective Zeheb wasn't thrilled about the timing. He was
going to miss the end of the show. And probably nothing
would pan out. "Look, it doesn't sound like it's going to
be much," he told his wife as he slid a tie under his collar.
"I'll be back in a little while."

Detective Zeheb and his Mercury Sable made it up to 210
South Belmont Avenue in less than half an hour. The lights
were off and there were no cars out front, so he kept driving.
Better to give the Richmond police a call before checking
it out anyway, and what do you know, he was just a few
blocks from Benedictine High, his own alma mater. He'd
radio in and have the local guys meet him at the school.

The house was lit up when the detective and his uniformed backup saw it next, and there was a white Ford
Taurus at the curb. A Richmond canine officer had heard
the call too, and he pulled up behind them with a dog in his
truck.

A hefty blond girl answered the door, and Detective
Zeheb asked her name.

"Dana Vaughan."

"Do you know somebody named Stacey?" He didn't
have a last name yet.

"Yeah, I do."

The questions came fast and steady. Zeheb employed a
"Dragnet"-style monotone for moments such as these. A
couple of the other cops waited on the sidewalk behind him,
and the rest in their cars.

"When was the last time you saw her?"

"Yesterday."

"Whose white car is this?"

"It's Tracy's."

"Can we talk to her?"

Dana turned enough to catch Tracy's petrified stare over her shoulder and looked back at the cop.

"Can I speak to you for a second?" Zeheb asked the second girl.

Tracy now stepped out into the dark and down the cement stairs to her car, trying very hard not to tower so precipitously over the detective.

"Oh my fucking God," said Turtle, making a dash for the window.

"Oh shit," said Dana.

They kneed up side-by-side on the sofa, hearts pounding, so that they could watch while Tracy opened her trunk. A couple more Richmond police cars arrived, and the guy with the pot figured this was a good time to leave. "I'm getting the fuck outta here," he muttered on his way to the back yard.

Then Zeheb was back in the front doorway.

"Look, is there somebody by the name of Turtle here?"

"Yeah, that's me."

"Can I speak to you?"

"Uh, sure."

"Let's take a walk."

Tracy was still standing over by the alleyway to Turtle's right when she stepped out onto the porch. Detective Zeheb steered Turtle left, past a row of disinterested faces behind squad car windows, and up to the corner of Parkwood Avenue.

"All right, so where's Stacey?"

Shit, no soft-pedaling here, thought Turtle.

"I don't know. She got out of the car because me and Tracy were makin' out. Around Byrd Park. We dropped her off. I don't know where the fuck she is."

"You haven't seen her all day?"

"Nope."

Zeheb adjusted his footing so as to indicate that he was getting serious now.

"Okay, look," he said. "You need to tell me the truth. I know the truth. Tracy just told me everything. I want the truth from you."

Now Turtle adjusted too. She took a step backward and crossed her arms—and the detective, well schooled in the police art of body language, found this a revealing pose. When she next spoke, he knew for sure that he had it right.

"That's when she told me that yeah, they did in fact beat her," he would say later.

Detective Zeheb instructed a young man and woman in Richmond uniforms to arrest Turtle, and they pushed her up against the side of their squad car, patted her down, and cuffed her. Then, from the back seat of the cruiser, she watched Tracy, all stooped and modest at the end of that alleyway, listening to Detective Zeheb. And now becoming enraged.

The problem was that Tracy had not told the truth that first time, but rather a different lie—that Stacey's last sighting was not in the doorway of the Tempo, under the trees in Byrd Park, but at the house itself. She'd left the house on foot, Tracy had reported, after Baby Shane's party. As the detective now unveiled his trap, Tracy tried to steal a look at Turtle through the closed window of the squad car.

The role of cooperative young adult—remorseful, recovered from any earlier misbehavior—was a natural for Tracy. It had helped her after countless fights; it had helped her with Karla, her mom, Turtle. Now, in a climactic flourish, she took a deep breath and confirmed the truth. And yes, she would take Detective Zeheb to the woods where she had last seen Stacey, as long as she didn't have to get out of the car. It was agreed. Turtle noticed with dismay that Tracy had free use of her arms until the very end, when she was given the passenger seat of the detective's Mercury Sable like an invited guest before disappearing into the night.

And then there was Domica—out of nowhere, like a ghost. Where had she been? And what was she doing sauntering onto this enemy-occupied block like an innocent? Run, man, run! Turtle wanted to shout.

Instead, she watched her elfin buddy, ears jangly with silver, that green watch still on her arm, as she made her way down the sidewalk in clear view of the police swarm. She scaled the front steps and was only inside for a matter of moments before her name came up.

Detective Mormando arrived on the scene just in time to escort Turtle and Domica to the old Richmond police headquarters on North Ninth Street.

Dana stayed home—"We can't promise you there won't be charges," Mormando told her, "but as of now, we're still investigating and we're not going to do anything." When the phone rang, she was the only one left at 210 South Belmont Avenue to answer it.

Hearing Stephanie's voice was too much for Dana, and she cried. "Tracy and Turtle and Mica . . . just got . . . taken away in handcuffs!" she told her. "I don't know what the fuck's goin' on. I gotta get outta here!"

Stephanie agreed to meet Dana down at the trailer at midnight. And then she turned, trembling, to her wise and reasonable girlfriend, who knew just what had to happen next.

They took the Tempo to the car wash at the Crown gas station off of Ironbridge Road, and let a series of giant, slurpy sponges wash away Marsh Field and Nash Road— and lull both passengers into feeling safe for a few minutes under a blanket of suds.

Cleaning the inside of the car was the hard part. They snaked the Crown station's vacuum hose around in there for a few minutes, and Claire noticed a Winnie-the-Pooh blanket, some clothes, and the tiny tip of a blade. There was also a black belt on the floor in back, about an inch wide, with a pattern of silver cutouts. The machine didn't begin to remove the shell of mud and blood that had dried on the

clear plastic floormats and along the edge of the dashboard.
That would take water and some powerful chemicals.

Back at Green Leigh, they parked where the Culls' driveway met Dottie Drive, and located a bottle of Armor-All
and some window cleaner in the kitchen; Cindy was asleep
and they were careful not to wake her. They had just washed
the dash and were starting on the windows when a dark,
unfamiliar sedan cruised slowly into view.

"Claire, start the car. Go," Stephanie whispered.

"No, let's see if it passes."

"No! Start the car! Now."

"Let's just see if it passes."

"Claire, start the car!"

Claire turned the key and put the Tempo into drive. They
had made it two houses down when the other car whipped
past, spun around in front, and slammed on its brakes.

Stephanie and Claire were taken up to the Chesterfield
County Jail and the car was towed to the County Academy
Garage.

22:

"There was no question of whether the body would be there or not. That wasn't what I was thinking. It was more along the lines of whether she was still alive or not. That's why we were beating the band coming back into the county, trying to get there as quick as we could."

—Detective Dave Zeheb

Detective Zeheb joined Carytown traffic with one hand on the wheel of his car and the other on his radio. Yep, he told Lieutenant Andy Scruggs, his immediate supervisor, he had one of them right here with him, and she was going to direct him to the spot where they'd left the girl. Yes, sir, he told Tommy Nowlin, the suspect said Beach Road, so what about meeting up at that bank just north of the turn? The parking lot there. From what Tracy Bitner was telling him, it couldn't be more than about two miles to the site.

The roads were typically clear for a Sunday night, but at one point there was a tie-up and Detective Zeheb flipped on his siren. Right away they were back up to speed. Between the detective's extensive updates on the radio and the wail of the siren, he and Tracy said barely a word to each other.

And then they were at the bank, and over in the parking lot, Lieutenant Scruggs and Sergeant Nowlin were waiting in their cars. After a brief exchange of words through open windows, they were off again, a high-speed, late-night convoy of three with Detective Zeheb and Tracy in the lead.

Beach Road was right there, a pretty street over gentle

rises that would have taken them into Pocahontas Park and a nice stretch of beach along Swift Creek Lake. Instead there was a quick turn left onto Nash Road. Now Tracy became more animated, peering through the detective's windshield toward the left side of the road. It was curvy and dark, and to her eyes, a repetitive pattern of indistinguishable, smallish homes and black clumps of forest. Tracy told Detective Zeheb that pretty soon there would be a little dirt road. She knew it would appear quickly after a thick fringe of trees that came all the way out to the road, but the lay of the land was never quite right. And then it seemed like the distance was too long.

"I think this is it," she told him at one point. But as the detective prepared to turn, she stopped him. "No, that's not it. Keep going."

The next time Tracy spoke, however, it was with absolute certainty.

"Right there," she said.

Detective Zeheb pivoted left and the other two cars followed, stopping just as quickly as they had turned. A simple metal gate blocked what looked like some kind of logging road. The rest of the trip would be on foot. There was some slamming of doors, and flashlights clicked on. Sergeant Nowlin would stay behind with Tracy.

The long-needled pines of the forest were a soft shroud: the detectives went around the gate and stepped into absolute silence and darkness. Detective Zeheb only noticed that it was muddy underfoot, a vaguely rutted trail of dirt and gravel punctuated by an occasional puddle. He didn't know where to look or what exactly he was going to find. It was instinct and the direction of the logging road, more than any specific instructions from Tracy, that sent the two detectives walking forward in a straight line.

And then they saw it: a spooky glow up ahead, white like chalk in the false light of their lamps. She was naked, or almost naked, and coated with pale, dry mud.

The pose that Stacey struck in her muddy bed, a three-quarters angle that put her left hip and shoulder above the rest of her body, arms folded under the right side of her head, suggested sleep. The film on her skin also might have tricked the mind into imagining some other reason for her rest here, because it disguised dozens of now-bloodless wounds. And her left arm blocked her throat from view.

There was no question for these men, however, standing right there over the still-wet, still-dark puddle of mud around her, that this was the body of someone who had endured a very slow, unimaginable death. Life was so thoroughly drained from her that she might have been carved from the palest of stone. And not even mud could hide the wide gash that ran nearly the length of her back, or her dry, blackened eyes and face.

So as not to disturb the crime scene, the detectives kept their distance, returning to their car radios to make some calls. Detective Dave Higgins and Lieutenant John Herndon of the Forensics Unit arrived right away and just as quickly put those 450 feet behind them.

A bright ribbon of plastic tape went up between the branches of the surrounding trees. Photographs were snapped, and the men bagged some things they found scattered around the body. A tiny piece of blade and a pair of sandals had been almost entirely submerged in the mud, and over to the side, in the brush, they recovered the orange plastic handle of a utility knife. There was also an eight-foot stick lined up along the length of the body that looked like it might have been used as a weapon.

Later, they would make molds of the various footprints found up and down that logging road and guess that the bare feet going in had belonged to the victim and the ones going out had been Tracy's.

Meanwhile, the body was removed to the offices of the medical examiner.

23:

I held my hands in front of me, as if they were bound at the wrists. Had Deborah locked her fingers together in a double fist and swung, and had the killer's reflex been to defensively raise his hands, in one of which he was holding the knife he had just used to murder Fred, then the hack to Deborah's left index finger made sense. Deborah ran like hell, and the killer, knocked off guard, shot her in the back.

—from *All That Remains*, by Patricia Cornwell

Devoted readers of Patricia Cornwell, Richmond's pre-eminent crime writer, tend to share a fascination with Marcella Fierro, the real-life chief medical examiner for the Commonwealth of Virginia. She's the inspiration for Kay Scarpetta, the fictional character with the same job who stars in and narrates most of Cornwell's books, and personally hunts down killers with an amazing ability to analyze human tissue—and the peculiar people she meets along the way.

Cornwell did computer work in the morgue for six years and then started trailing Fierro around her job, chatting her way through autopsies and filling notebooks with the nuances of FBI tactics sessions. The arrangement leaves the authenticity of Cornwell's research rarely in doubt; Fierro is purported to proofread her books just in case.

Fierro herself is a tiny, no-nonsense technician who favors plain skirt suits and blends right into the background until she speaks. Which she does plainly, but with a gleam in her eyes that betrays not just intelligence but great interest. Her office conducts 5,600 postmortems—including 2,700 full autopsies—a year. In murder cases, she lists every cut and abrasion, every bruise and fracture, and makes an analysis about the cause and timing of each. Disputed points may send her off in one particular direction of inquiry, but she has theories for everything that she doesn't completely understand and when she shows up to testify at trial, not even the sharpest defense lawyer can distract her.

When Stacey Hanna's body arrived, so youthful that her teeth were fitted with braces and so slight as to weigh just 126 pounds, Fierro's staff set about removing the muddy scum in which she had been found, the scrap of bikini underwear, and the small piece of string that the victim appeared to have worn on her right ankle as jewelry. All the better to view the patchwork of gashes and bruises and deep scrapes and to move as quickly as possible to the matter of her cause of death: specifically, whether it was more likely the muddy liquid seeping into Stacey's lungs or the drainage out—the bleeding—that had killed her.

It was clear right away to Dr. Fierro that Stacey might have died as late as Sunday afternoon—might have continued breathing for hours and hours after she was left behind in that puddle. But she needed to know what it was that had finally ended her life.

The victim's blood loss was so extreme that her organs were "pale." And yet the water had clearly been a major factor: There was so much of it, not just in her lungs but in her stomach as well, where Dr. Fierro discovered 150 brownish milliliters.

The medical examiner took the extra time to be sure about this important question. The victim's former friends would claim a broad variety of assaults: finding a trail between one particular injury or kind of injury and the body's ultimate surrender was no small matter. There were so many questions to answer. How significant, for instance, was this throat wound? And what about the various punctures—

surely not all inflicted with the same instrument?

Nobody—not even the battery of defense lawyers in this case who would need Fierro's take before they could adequately plan out their cases—was going to rock the medical examiner's solid, leakproof boat. There would be tests and more tests until her autopsy report was months behind schedule.

Meanwhile, the injuries that didn't as directly threaten Stacey's life were also of concern to Dr. Fierro, inflicted as they were in such great number and over such a long period of time. She counted over 65 cuts and had rarely seen anything quite so consistently shallow: Many went no farther than an eighth of an inch into Stacey's flesh. Even the two slices that ran along the length of her back for more than 14 inches were just half an inch deep.

Something blunt had slammed repeatedly into the girl's skull but also her arms, legs, hands, and feet. One blow had fractured the bridge of her nose. And on the back of her left shoulder, Dr. Fierro found a strange series of dots, inflicted perhaps by something sharp embedded in a larger instrument that they had been beating her with. Other abrasions suggested that Stacey had been dragged.

Someone had also carved a series of long, crisscrossing lines along the front of her right leg. They would seem, not just to the untrained eye but to many of the forensic experts involved in this case along the way, to be wide, sweeping capital letters spelling out the word "LIAR"—the ultimate tattoo.

24:

"I just didn't know what to do. I didn't know whether
to try to help her, or to be with them, or to . . . I mean,
I was just so scared, and I just wanted, all I knew was
I wanted her to shut up."

—Turtle

"Who the fuck said something?" Domica whispered to
Turtle when they were left alone for a minute in a corridor
at Richmond police headquarters, cuffed and sweaty, a di-
minutive, scowling pair.

"I don't know," Turtle said. And it was true. If she was
less surprised by their predicament than Domica, having herself rushed off to blab, she was quite in the dark about which
of the signals sent out into Sunday afternoon had reached
the genuine snitch.

"I've been sleeping all day," Domica told Turtle.
"What'd y'all do?"

The cops returned before she could answer. And there
wouldn't be another free moment like that—not between
Tracy and Stephanie down with the county police either—
until it was too late and everyone had spent a long time in
front of video cameras.

The isolation of the hallways, cells, and interrogation
rooms where the four waited and then spoke and then waited
some more that night left everybody with a lot to guess at.
Allegiances shifted in their minds. What were the others
saying? Was there blame being misassigned? Or protection

lovingly bestowed? It was a first taste of the loneliness and paranoia of the coming months.

What they could certainly have used was the legal advice that all four of them declined. Somebody to explain, for example, that while it may make sense at the time to cover for your dearest friends and heap their troubles on somebody less dear—just in case they're doing it for you—what if they're not?

Until a bailiff rolls a video monitor up in front of the jury box at your murder trial, a circuitous route to the truth probably looks like any other route to the truth. Especially to four very young, very confused women who were nowhere near explaining—even to themselves—why this had happened. Who instead were finding out, as Sunday turned into Monday, that Stacey was in fact dead, and they were all being charged with murder.

TURTLE

The first of the interviews was Turtle's, a slow, chatty session in a room with a single table and two wooden chairs. It took a long time to find out what Turtle really knew because at first she chose to give Domica all the bloodiest moments, so as to protect not just herself but Tracy too.

Turtle's afternoon ambiguity about Tracy was miraculously gone. Now she told the detective that Tracy was her "one and only love." It was as if, starting at the beginning as Detective Mormando asked, she had stumbled onto the memory of being so mad at Stacey, and was once again making a choice between them.

"Well," she began, "Stacey said she was all in love with me and stuff like that. And she kept trying to say things to break me and Tracy up . . . And I kept telling her, 'I can't be with you. I can't be with you. I'm in love with Tracy.' "

That was constant, she said. The last straw was Saturday night when Stacey tried to bury Tracy's teary declaration of love for Turtle under a big lie.

"And I was like, what the hell. It was like, I'm gonna fuckin', I want to fuckin' beat her ass. And everybody else was like, 'Yeah, we're gonna beat her ass.' Just, you know, messing around. You know, people done that to *me*. You know, I get a couple bruises or something like that."

The reality, out at some place near the airport, was quite different. Turtle said that Domica came at Stacey with her belt and the others joined in.

"Well, I hit her twice in her head," she said.

"With what?" asked the detective.

"My fist. Just my fist. Um, I kicked her, you know."

The blades that came out next drew almost as much blood from Turtle as Stacey. Then, "Mica was walking behind us and she picked up this cinder block and she was like, 'Aw, bitch,' and she just threw it."

Detective Mormando asked, "When she hit her with the cinder block, at this point was she unconscious?"

"No," said Turtle. "She was still like, 'Why are you doing this to me? Why are you doing this?' And we were like, 'Just shut up and get in the car.' "

Or rather, the trunk. Arriving at the logging road many long minutes later, they pulled her out and Turtle thought they were leaving her there. And so she smacked her around one last time.

"I kept saying, 'Come on, let's get out of here. Let's just go.' And so was Tracy. Tracy was like, 'Let's get out of here.' Mica was like, 'Why are you gonna do that?' And she was just kicking her."

But instead they hoisted her between them and walked into the dark. At some point, Turtle got her sneaker stuck in the mud.

"I panicked and I was like, Oh my God. I was freaking out. Because, I mean I am not a violent person at all. And I just don't know. I blacked out. I didn't realize what I had done or what I was doing until after I had done it . . . I just remember running to the car."

Mormando knew from Dana that something else had happened down there: Somebody had cut her throat and somebody had stabbed her in the back with a stick. And his own hunch was that it was Domica, which jibed nicely with Turtle's fleeting efforts to shield Tracy.

"Did Mica ever talk about cutting her throat?" the detective asked.

"I'm trying to think . . . I remember at one point Mica saying, 'I want your heart.' . . .''

"Do you think Mica wanted to kill her?"

"She said, 'I want to stab you in your chest.' I remember her saying that but I don't—''

"I need to know who did that [cut her throat]."

"Mica."

DOMICA

Domica waited her turn, barefoot and cuffed to a chair, in a big room full of computers and desks that were separated from each other by a maze of low partitions. When Turtle emerged from her interrogation, Domica caught sight of her quickly before being escorted inside to take her place. It was 1:40 a.m. when Detective Mormando sat down with his second charge.

Domica was more brazen about lying. She was also strikingly insightful about Stacey's needs—seeing even beyond the dead girl's desire to have Turtle to herself.

"Stacey, she has a problem with trying to get everybody to turn against everybody," she told the detective. "And it was like she was telling sob stories and lies, trying to fit in with everybody else. And everybody was just unhappy about it. Especially Tracy and Turtle."

On the trip to pick up Robyn that night, she went on, they all decided they'd had enough, and they drove into the county and started beating her up.

"What did you beat her with?" asked Detective Mormando.

"I used my foot. I just used my foot and hand. That was it. And then somehow when I looked she had a slice down

"Turtle" Tibbs had been a fixture on Richmond, Virginia's teenage lesbian scene since she was 14. (Robyn Thirkill)

The best friend: Robyn Thirkill was Turtle's "butch brother." (Sarah Franklin)

The house: the place they rented at 210 South Belmont Avenue, smack in the middle of bohemian Carytown, always drew a crowd. (Sally Chew)

The driver: Stephanie Cull (right) was always ferrying somebody to work or reclining in the living room, to the dismay of her girlfriend, Claire Watson (left). (Cindy Cull)

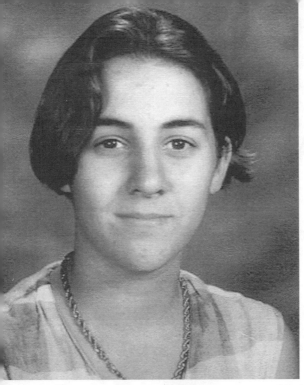

The new girl: When Stacey Hanna came to town in July, she fell hard for Turtle — who was not quite done with Tracy. (Brookville High School)

Stacey waitressed on the Annabel Lee riverboat and struggled clumsily for three weeks to keep Turtle and Tracy apart. (Sally Chew)

Marsh Field, a small clearing next to the county airport, was the place selected for Stacey's ass-kicking. (Sally Chew)

But the assault was finally played out on a remote, muddy trail off Nash Road. (Sally Chew)

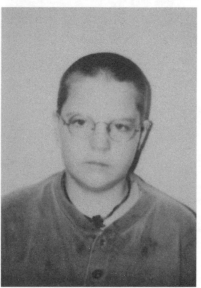

The cops had no trouble tracking down Stacey's murderers — because one of them squealed.
(All photos Chesterfield VA County Police)

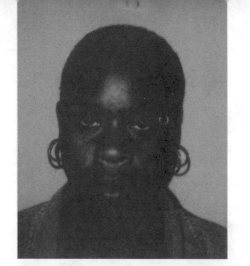

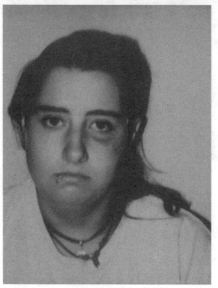

STACEY L HANNA

3
29
79

7
27
97

Stacey's mom put up a bright white marker at the turnoff to the murder scene. (Sally Chew)

her back, and, matter of fact, she had like two slices down her back. And I think she had one on her side or her neck or somewhere. That was when I panicked. I was, like, forget it. I'm leaving.''

And when Stacey was thrashing around in the trunk, she said, ''That was when Kelley and Tracy were saying that we gotta kill her.

''So we went through a gate opening, we went to a dirt road. Out somewhere in the boonies. I helped Tracy and Kelley get her out of the trunk. And after that I just got in the car and sat there. I left it alone after that. It was like cars riding past while we were sitting right there in the car waiting on them.''

Waiting on them? At this point, Mormando was starting to pick up fiction in her voice. And so he told her that he didn't believe her so far, and that now was her chance to get serious.

Domica listened and said ''Umhum'' a lot, and then she seemed to switch gears entirely. She explained that she had expected the interrogation to reach this moment; she knew the detective would call her bluff and that she would have to say what had really happened. ''Anybody gonna do what they can do to get theirself out of trouble,'' she told him.

She tried to tell the truth now, starting very small. Her interlocutor listed the items just picked up from the grass at Marsh Field in the last hours: rings, brown hair clippings, a chunk of a cinder block with some blood on it. And she admitted to cutting Stacey's hair.

And then, yes, she threw the cinder block. ''But it did not hit her. It missed her. The cinder block missed her. Her hand was like, no—It was her leg. The cinder block went over her leg, hit the ground.''

She hovered on that margin, just this side of the real story, coming up with the fuzzy idea, for example, that Stacey had agreed to get in the trunk. And then she went briefly overboard.

''I slit her throat,'' she said.

''You slit her throat,'' Mormando repeated.

"Okay now, that's where I draw the line, because I did not slit her throat. Here . . . Tracy slit her throat."

"Why do you think Turtle would tell me that you cut her [throat]? To protect Tracy?"

"I guess so, because her and Tracy are so in love. I guess so. But I did not cut her [throat]. I stabbed her in her chest."

Domica was the only one of the four who felt that there had been a group decision to kill Stacey. Perhaps, growing up in a family of such softspoken people, she was more skilled in communicating without words. She knew by osmosis when they had made up their minds.

Now Detective Mormando moved on to the strategizing that had gone on while Stacey was in the trunk.

"So you decided at this point you wanted to kill her."

"Yeah."

"Ok. Do you have any idea how you were gonna kill her?"

"No. We had no idea."

"You had no idea how you were gonna kill her?"

"We just wanted to do it. We did not know how we were gonna do it."

And then they found themselves with Stacey at that muddy spot on the logging road.

"That was when we started scrambling, trying to get her to die or whatever. And um—"

"I'm sorry?"

"We were scrambling to try to get her to quiet down."

TURTLE

Mormando, now equipped with Domica's story about Tracy being the throat-cutter, called Turtle in for a second interview, which he launched with a formidable lecture:

". . . I'm telling you right now, if you don't tell me who did that to her, then you might as well have the knife in your hand yourself . . . I think you're afraid to tell me. Because you feel like you're rolling on somebody. But you know, friendship goes a long way. And then it doesn't go a long way. It's up to the person who did it to own up to it . . ."

He now swayed into buddy mode, but was clearly confused about which corner of this love triangle was Turtle's:

"I've been in that situation with a girl before. Where somebody has come between me and my girlfriend and I want to kick the crap out of them and all that . . . And I know how you felt, and it just got out of hand, and I don't think you're a bad person.

"But I don't want you to get in trouble for something that you didn't do. And I know you didn't cut her throat, but I know you know who did . . . It was Tracy, wasn't it?"

"Yeah."

Neither Domica nor Turtle knew until later that Stacey's body had been found.

"You think she's dead now?" Detective Mormando asked Turtle.

"God, I hope not . . . but . . . I mean, we kicked her so much. And she's so little. . . . We sat around the car. And we were like, Oh my God, you know, I kicked her so much. I got blood on my shoe."

"So what's been going on today? Were you glad that she was gone?"

"No."

"I mean, you been so pissed off at her 'cause she's been coming between you and Tracy. Are you finally glad that, you know, that she's gone?"

"No. I mean, I kept telling her I wanted her to move back to Lynchburg. Because, you know, this wasn't her place right now. And she was like, 'I love you so much.' And, I mean, she just did so much and it just drove me crazy."

"Who is the main instigator in this whole thing do you think?"

"I was the first one that said that I want to fucking beat her up."

"All right. But who do you think took it to the next level? Mica or Tracy?"

"We were all kind of feeding off each other . . . [But] after I got cut I was like, 'Y'all, you know, I got cut twice. This is not fucking fun anymore. You know, I'm not having fun at all.' "

DOMICA

Turtle had casually mentioned that Domica was wearing a watch that she'd taken from Stacey—which would make this even more serious a crime than Detective Mormando had thought. Under Virginia law, you can get the death penalty for certain combinations of murder and robbery.

"Did you think you had any right to that watch?" he now asked Domica in their second session together.

She had no idea what he was talking about.

"Excuse me?"

Detective Mormando was quite struck by Domica's last words that night, and in fact found them so evil that he would mention them to reporters, slightly out of context.

"Nobody deserves to die, but it was just one of those times," Domica told him.

"One of those times for what?"

"When somebody had to die . . . That's all. I mean, I regret it. I'm sorry for it. I know we can't bring her back or nothing like that but, I mean, it'll stick in my head. Every day. You know what I'm saying? Because it was like one minute she was a friend and the next minute she was a, what you want to call it, not an enemy but, like an associate or somebody you just say Hi and Bye to. And it was like the next minute she was a victim."

Now, in the pre-dawn hours, Turtle and Domica were allowed to speak to each other—and to call home. Fingerprinting was next, but then there was some more waiting. And that's when they got their first inkling that this nightmare of theirs was a big deal not just to them but to the world, or to Richmond, at least.

"Oh, well, basically it's a lesbian triangle," some police officer was saying into a telephone. "There's a body, and we've found it."

He was talking to a reporter: He was telling everybody!

Stacey Hanna's killers were the real loudmouths that night, however—and in the days to come. The deputies at headquarters who put Turtle and Domica through "processing" and pressed their fingertips into ink pads were stunned at their banter. These girls were shameless; they didn't want lawyers and then here they were engaged in a calm discussion about a murder.

Daylight was on its way when the paperwork was done. The pair would be moved down to the county in the morning, but for now they were given cells for the night, across a room from each other with only bars between them. Domica smoked a lot of cigarettes. The prisoner in the next cell went a little bug-eyed about the questions going back and forth. Such as, "Do you know if she's dead or not?"

"Mica, I'm scared," Turtle said at one point.

"I know. It's gonna be all right, though. Just tell the truth—wherever you go."

"All right."

"We gotta stick together."

Then Domica asked, "Do you know where Stephanie or Tracy is?"

"Well, they took Tracy somewhere."

"What do you mean, They took Tracy somewhere?"

"I don't know."

"Do you think she turned us in?"

"No . . . I don't know."

TRACY

After Detective Zeheb's excursion down that logging road, he was full of questions. He got a more precise fix from

Tracy on which Dumpster she'd put those clothes in at
Matchpoint apartments (that first search had turned up nothing). But mostly what he wanted to understand was the romantic tangle behind the display of cruelty he had just
witnessed. It was about three miles back to the Chesterfield
County police station, where he and Tracy settled into a long
talk, starting with the four-way teenage love story that had
consumed these girls so gravely.

"All right. You and Turtle, or Kelley, were girlfriends
with a commitment at one time?"

"Umhum. And then we broke up. And I started seeing
Sandy."

"And then she started seeing Stacey, is that it?"

"Umhum."

Saturday night was "kind of weird" because all four of
them were going to try and socialize together. "I was like,
Great, somebody is gonna feel awkward. And it was cool
'cause, you know, we all just hung out.

"Me and Sandy had been drinking earlier. At a cookout.
Then we went to Baby Shane's and, you know, we were all
drinking or whatever . . . Went over there about a couple
hours. Came back. And it was great. It was cool."

Except that Stacey was a pain in the butt: Tracy now
feigned an effort to explain what exactly she was doing that
annoyed them so, but instead she skipped right past her own
teary "sugar room" declaration of love for Turtle, and Stacey's subsequent lie. She chose instead to focus on Friday's
conflict about Stacey pretending that Sharon had a crush on
her.

Either Tracy was consciously trying to appear extraneous
to the conflict—or she had actually convinced herself that
it was *only* for Turtle that she and Domica and Stephanie
had trooped out to Marsh Field less than 24 hours earlier.

Detective Zeheb could not possibly have understood a
motive in her chaotic summary about Sharon, and he didn't
try any further to decipher the subtleties of their teenage
rancor. He got the gist of it, though: Early Sunday morning,
the girls decided they'd had enough of Stacey's storytelling.

"Everybody was like, 'We're gonna teach Stacey a lesson 'cause she lies so much,'" Tracy told him. "'She switches stories around, blah blah blah blah.' I'm like, all right. Okay. Cool . . . You know, just a good ass-whipping. And you know it's nothing wrong with that."

Tracy had heard of a place down by the Chesterfield airport, and so they all got in the car and Tracy gave directions to a small field. "There was a driveway and there was a truck. And it was like a little building there. No windows or anything. Looked like a little shop or something. I don't even know . . .

"Next thing I know, Mica and Turtle are just—Mica is over here and Turtle like *bam bam*, just started kicking her. I was going, 'God, guys, get off. Stop.' And then it was like, Oh my God, they're gonna kill her . . .

"I didn't punch her. I didn't kick her. I didn't touch her. All I did was cut her with the razor blade."

Domica, though, picked up a cinder block and threw it at her. "When I saw the cinder block hit her head," Tracy went on, now dabbing at her eyes and nose with a tissue, "she was like laying on her back. And she's, I guess, in a fetus position."

"Is she still crying? Is she screaming at y'all?"

"She's, um, she's not really crying. She's just, 'Oh stop, guys,' you know. Not really screaming like bloody murder or anything like that."

But later, when they left Stacey there at Marsh Field and then came back, the plan was to actually kill her, right? Detective Zeheb was looking for premeditation: "Y'all were back 'cause y'all were scared. Cause you had hurt her pretty good, and you knew that you had to kill her because she was gonna talk. Is that what you're saying?"

"Yeah. That never came out of my mouth. I—that was not out of my mouth. At all."

"Okay."

"It could have been Stephanie. I don't know . . ."

"But it's a fair statement that everybody was thinking that that's what had to be done. Okay. Including you?"

"Including me . . ."

"Let me ask you this, Tracy. When y'all left Marsh Field and she was in the trunk and y'all were driving around, what did y'all talk about then? . . ."

" 'We gotta get rid of her or she's gonna rat us out. We're gonna go to jail.' "

"When you say you gotta get rid of her, you meant—"

"Like just toss her somewhere. Where nobody could find her. I didn't think we'd kill her. I never had planned on killing her. I never even thought of, like, touching her."

"But you said earlier—"

"Everybody knows I'm a buncha talking. That's all I was gonna be. I had planned on sitting down there, just shooting the shit. Talking everything out. Like, 'Why did you say this?' You know? 'Don't be saying shit like that' or whatever."

"Things just went bad."

"Things went real bad."

Bad as in throat-cutting and stabbing: Tracy described the flurry of crude knifework at their final stop under the pines and then she described seeing Turtle: "She was, like, she came around and she, like, grabbed her throat."

"Turtle did? Grabbed her throat for what reason?"

" 'Cause Stacey was still breathing, and she was like, 'Help! Help!' Trying to scream. I put my hand over her mouth, and then that's when Turtle stuck her hand [out] and like grabbed [her]."

STEPHANIE

Claire and Stephanie got to the Chesterfield County police station long after Detective Zeheb had finished with Tracy. He sat down with Claire first, while Stephanie waited with her ankles cuffed to a metal ring in the floor of another interrogation room. Claire stuck to the story about Stacey getting out of the car on her own—and was sent home.

The detective offered Stephanie a cigarette and then

failed in his search around the police station to find her one before turning the video recorder back on. Stephanie assumed that her well-behaved girlfriend had told the truth, and so she jumped right into the real story, starting with a detailed explanation of Stacey's ill-fated campaign:

"She had told Turtle that Tracy said she wanted Sandy to spend the night. And that she didn't love Turtle, and she was playing Turtle, and all this stuff. And she got Turtle all upset about that. When in actuality, Tracy had said the opposite. That she loved Turtle."

"Do you think she was trying to split Turtle and Tracy?" Detective Zeheb asked.

"I don't know what she was trying to do . . . She had said the weirdest stuff. I have no idea what was going through her head. But they decided they wanted to beat her up. And I was, like, 'Okay.' And Joe had no idea what was going on. I tried to get her not to go."

With that exception, she told the detective, she had been mostly a follower that night. There was less concrete evidence of this than she would have liked—and she didn't go so far as to say that she was afraid of what the others would do to her if she stopped them or drove away. Her paralysis was just as easily interpreted as indifference.

Stephanie said she had pocketed one of the boxcutters on her way out the door, and Detective Zeheb wanted to know why:

"Is it fair to say that y'all took these razors because you figured that she was gonna get a pretty good one for making everybody mad?"

"I don't know."

"You don't walk around with razors in your pocket all the time, do you?"

"No. Definitely not."

At Marsh Field, Stephanie followed cues from the others, she told Detective Zeheb—at one point Tracy even told her to come over and help. But the injuries she inflicted with her shoes, she said, were minor. And she had objected to the idea of driving off and leaving Stacey lying there all alone in the dark.

"So then, um, she was in the trunk," Stephanie went on, "and we all got back in the car. We turned around and we were driving down the road. And she was banging on the trunk. So we pulled over and I think Mica got out. To see what she wanted. And I think that's when she asked us to take her to a hospital. So we were driving and trying to decide, you know, what we should do. If we should take her to a phone. If we should take her to a hospital."

Zeheb asked her, "Isn't it true that y'all talked about, 'Look, we need to kill her because—' "

"At this point it wasn't down to that yet. We were still driving down Cogbill Road. Trying to figure out what we should do with her. When she asked for us to take her to a phone, she was like, 'I swear I won't say anything. I won't mention anybody's names. I'll go back to Lynchburg' . . . And somebody was, like, 'Well, you know, why should we trust her? Why should we trust that she wouldn't say our names?' . . .

"I think Tracy said something about cutting her tongue out. So that she wouldn't talk."

"Okay," the detective said, "you're driving around and you're talking about it. And you knew that you went over the line."

"Yeah. And I—"

"You couldn't turn back."

"I really didn't want them to kill her. I really didn't. I didn't know what to do. I really didn't know what to do."

"But you knew you went over the line. You couldn't turn back."

"I mean, I knew it had gone way too far. Yeah. But I never thought we should kill her. Ever. That thought never entered my mind. I thought they were just gonna beat her up a little bit. You know, take her back home and that was gonna be it."

"Did you cut her?" Zeheb asked right then.

"I cut her twice." Once on her leg in the trunk and again

at the pipe gate, just before the others walked her off into the woods. That was where her first-hand understanding of Stacey's wounds came to an end.

"I got back to the car, and I sat down. And maybe about five minutes later I saw a lighter flash . . . But that's all that I could see, you know. It was like pitch black. And I don't know how long they were out there. It seemed like a really long time. It seemed like forever. I heard a couple screams."

25:

When the Sunday dinner hour wound down over at Ruby Tuesday, Robyn had one thing on her mind: beer. She called the house at 11:15 to see if someone could please help her with the bewitching approach of midnight. Dana told her only that she was on her own with the beer, and "If you get some, you better get a lot."

The news, when Dana finally laid it out for her in person, switched Robyn into automatic. It was never apparent from the outside when Robyn was on edge; she hovered unemotionally above any difficult scene. And so she did that night. She knew, without feeling it yet, that this was the end of something: this was a disaster that would change everybody's lives.

It was Dana who wasn't facing the facts.

"I knew Stacey was dead," Robyn would say later. "Just because it had been a day since she was missing. And then Dana kept on denying it, and she kept going, 'They haven't found her yet, haven't found her yet, haven't found her yet.' "

Dana and her annoying denial—or was she hiding something?—were gone quickly, though; she was spending the night with a friend. And Robyn was left alone in the empty house with her questions. She was on the phone with Monique—they were back in touch again, but not really dating—when a detective clicked in on call waiting. He needed her to find some ID for Stacey, and he sounded pretty serious about it.

"Put the phone down and go look," he told her. "I'll wait."

Robyn spent ten sweaty minutes among the indecipherable piles in Turtle's room. She pulled at wads of fabric and groped around for hard, wallet-like shapes. There were photographs and boxes and cd's galore, but nothing with Stacey's name on it. She returned to the cop on the phone with empty hands.

"I'm really looking, but I can't find anything," she told him. "There's so much stuff."

Yeah, well, the cop wouldn't take that for an answer. "We're going to send some people over to help you look," he told Robyn.

Monique, still hanging on the other line, decided to come over too, and that turned out to be a good thing because several long, quiet hours went by with nary a police officer in sight. It was almost dawn when somebody finally showed.

There were two of them: two detectives in street clothes who weren't so interested in ID anymore but seemed to have something just as specific in mind. They were going to look down that alley, they said.

"Can we take these?" one of them inquired about the muddy Airwalks still drying by the front door and quite invisible to the naked and unsuspecting eye.

"Have at it," Robyn told him. "Whatever you need to do."

The girls also handed over the fruits of a second attempt to sort out Stacey's belongings upstairs: photographs, some letters addressed to Stacey, and four small bottles of eye drops that, in fact, happened to be Tracy's.

"We'll put these with the rest of her things," one of the cops said—his words striking down Robyn's last hope that Stacey was still breathing somewhere.

A couple of uniformed cops joined the detectives out in the alleyway, and they seemed to find what they were looking for. At one point they took some oversized Ziploc bags from the trunk of the car and put on latex gloves. Robyn and Monique watched through the blinds in the living room.

This was taking a long time and Robyn still didn't know where the girls were.

"I don't know about you," Robyn asked one of the detectives on a brief trip inside, "but I got a whole buncha friends missing. Can you tell me something?"

"I understand," he said. "I'm sorry, I know you're upset. But I really can't give you any information."

Robyn and Monique were exhausted by the time the plastic bags had been packed away and the officers had disappeared into early morning traffic—and yet too wired to sleep the hour or so before Monique's morning computer class. So they headed downtown to the Third Street Diner in time to share a "first call" pitcher at six a.m.

At 7:30, Robyn was still awake, but now stretched out on her bed with her eyes closed, praying to drift off. Then the phone rang.

"Robyn, what's going on?" Doris Tibbs was crying and sloppy. She had heard from Turtle at about five. With just enough information to drive her crazy. "Did they kill somebody, Robyn?"

"I don't know, Doris. Please don't ask me that. All I know is they're in jail," she said.

"They're chargin' 'em with murder," Doris said then, and it was the first Robyn had heard about that—although by now it was not exactly a surprise.

Next came Tracy's grandmother.

"I heard she was in jail," Robyn told her.

And then Tracy's mother, asking, "What's going on?"

"Well, I know they're in jail. Some cop called to ask me if Tracy lived here."

Robyn was wondering if she had it in her to break the mindblowing news of the day to every parent and grandparent in town. Since when was it her job to make these people cry? Then again, who else were they going to turn to? Robyn grew resigned to missing a full night's sleep and settled in to the latest incarnation of her Dad gig.

"They're being charged with murder," she finally told Tracy's mom.

Stephanie's grandmother seemed to know what was going on. She called just to get some kind of confirmation, and Robyn obliged.

Tracy's mom phoned a second time, to say that Tracy's step-dad was coming to pick up that big white Taurus at the curb, and took the chance to vent.

"I can't believe those girls did this!" she nearly shouted. She was angry, but it was as if she were talking about something she'd read in the paper, about somebody else's daughter. "I can't believe it!"

It was early afternoon when a *Richmond Times–Dispatch* reporter named Mark Bowes knocked on the door. "Do you want to comment?" he asked. Robyn had never been so tired or had so many people after her for something she knew nothing about. She told him No and closed the door again.

The next time she opened it, it was so that she and Monique could escape the phone and the news—and the house; it was clear by now that 210 South Belmont was going to be everybody's first stop for explanations. But right there in the middle of the porch, poised to knock, was a Channel 12 crew with a camera that now recorded the expressions of two snarling young women on the shaded front porch of a red house.

What actually appeared on the 6 o'clock news that night, however, was a shot of Robyn and Monique climbing into Monique's truck and pulling out into the street, because during the entire walk from the house, Monique had her middle finger in the air. "Can I fuckin' sue you for this?" Monique asked. "Because I think you're invading my privacy."

The reporters wandered around speaking to neighbors after that and didn't pick up anything very shocking. The man next door—he was married to the lady who bummed cigarettes—told the camera that they were "nice girls, regular girls."

Even so, 210 South Belmont Avenue itself became quickly and irrevocably tied to the murder in the public mind, and by extension its inhabitants' unsupervised, lesbian youth. Which, in turn, caused embarrassment around Carytown and the Fan that this rare spotlight on gay life was such an ugly one.

Robyn endured the brunt of both: "It was pretty much more than anybody could handle," she would remember. It would be a matter of days before Robyn decided to move back in with her folks up in Dale City.

When Sandy got home from work on Monday morning, it was a little before 8:30 and there was a message from Tracy on her machine. The call had come at 7. She could tell that Tracy had been crying.

"Yo, man, I'm in jail," the message said. And then Tracy seemed to snicker slightly, as if to marvel at the ridiculous fix she had gotten herself into. She became serious again just as fast, though. "It's not funny," she said. And finally, "Talk to you later."

The real state of things didn't hit Sandy, though, until the news came on at noon and she saw Tracy's picture.

Cindy Cull, Stephanie's mother, went to work as usual on Monday morning and parked her car in the lot at the Medical College of Virginia as if it were just any July day. Wondering where Stephanie was, certainly, but not worrying about it. After all, she'd been with Claire the last Cindy knew. "I didn't worry when she was with Claire," she would say later. "Claire's such a good girl."

The bad news—she'd thought she'd had bad news before, what with Stephanie's arthritis, the car accident, her own stroke—came from her boss. Cindy would remember that hearing his words, delivered carefully and deliberately as they were, was like being hit in the face with a baseball bat. Stephanie was in jail for murder, he told her. Someone had heard about it on television or the radio and phoned him.

Cindy, generally one of the quietest people in the place, began to wail. She was inconsolable, especially when somebody pulled up the internet and there it was again: Stephanie Cull, arrested with three other girls in the murder of Stacey Hanna.

But from the beginning, the tragedy of the murder itself loomed as large to Cindy as the discovery of what was happening to her child. When one of her office mates vowed, "We're going to get a good attorney," Cindy didn't want to hear about it. It seemed to her that the disaster of the moment was that an 18-year-old girl had been horribly murdered.

"That child's mother is trying to pick out something to wear at her funeral," she scolded.

In fact, there would be a "good attorney"—Richmond's best, if you believe the advertising running endlessly on television and even printed on paper table mats at area restaurants. The Cull family was the only one of the four to avoid a court-appointed lawyer. Cindy's good friend Melanie charmed Joe Morrissey into trimming his usual high fees. And then she pulled together a group of MCV faculty members willing to loan it to Cindy.

It was of no concern now that Morrissey's reputation had been sullied again and again in recent years by scandalous clients and his own collection of contempt charges earned on their behalf; when Joe Morrissey went to court, he had a habit of winning.

A hundred and fifty miles away, in Debbie Parker's office south of Lynchburg, the news was slower to arrive. It was after 5 p.m. on Monday when it hit the courthouse basement. Debbie was reviewing cases with her boss when the phone rang. Her secretary tried to take a message but the caller insisted on being put through.

"Hello?" Debbie answered.

A therapist friend gave her name and asked, "Who's with you?"

Then she came right out with it: "Stacey Hanna got murdered over the weekend."

"What?"

Debbie sorted through the words in that sentence and even before she understood them, believed them, she was adrift. It was shock, to be sure, but mostly it was the familiar—if this time more deeply felt—despair of her work.

After 15 years at this job, handling 20 cases at a time, checking out as many as 70 complaints a month, why did this one hurt so much? She'd seen babies burned alive. It's what she did—she protected kids—and yet it was her failures that came screaming back at her now. What flashed in her mind was how Stacey had been mad at her all the time, furious and sad all at once, brooding right here again and again, sometimes with her forehead resting miserably on the top of Debbie's desk.

And then Debbie remembered a call from Stacey years before, when a boy whom Debbie had been working with had hanged himself on Christmas.

"Debbie? Stacey." That rough-edged voice could only mean something was wrong. But no, not this time.

"Just calling to say I'm sorry," Stacey had said. "I saw you talking to him at the school."

Debbie had only known Stacey to think of herself—a full load, surely—but she was quite touched the day that Stacey had seemed to notice Debbie's own pain and reached out to her.

"Who told you this?" Debbie now asked this messenger of impossible, ghastly tidings.

"I can tell you it's true."

"She called me to come get her," was all Debbie could say—and it would be her refrain that night.

The caller, who didn't know what Debbie was talking about, kept going with her story.

"She was stabbed. That's all I know."

Somehow Debbie returned the receiver of her office phone to its cradle. A friend showed up at the office, took possession of her car keys, and drove her home. And still she could only say one thing:

"She called me to come get her."

When the police told Dana over the phone that Stacey's mother, Cathy Wilson, was going to be coming by the house on Tuesday to get Stacey's things, she didn't really know what to expect. Mostly she was petrified—and furious when Robyn ducked out to pick up some garbage bags at the store.

"Don't leave me alone with her!" Dana begged. "She'll be here any time!"

When Robyn got back, Cathy was up in Turtle's room—Stacey's room—with two other women and a man. They all had bags in their hands, and Dana was directing them to Stacey's things and hanging around to help distinguish one pair of jeans or stack of cd's from another.

Dana knew Cathy—a slim, wiry woman with dark, dense eyebrows and puffy blond hair—from her short time in Lynchburg, and also from Stacey's stories about their stormy relationship. She had been afraid of seeing her today for two reasons: Because Dana had been in that car—and here she was running around Richmond unpunished; and because, as Stacey's link to this group, she was Cathy's most visible reminder of *the lesbian question*.

It was an issue that had haunted Cathy's relationship with Stacey when she was alive and would haunt it again as the lawyers and reporters looking into this murder became matter-of-fact about Stacey's sexual preference—at the time of her death. Cathy was quite insistent that her daughter had not been gay.

But when the older woman was done upstairs and heading out, she told Dana goodbye warmly, and she was nice to Robyn too. Her friends were already in the car again when she approached the masculine-looking black girl in the living room whom she knew as the household elder.

"I realize that you didn't have anything to do with this," she told Robyn. "I realize that this must be hard for you

too. It was a good effort for you to try and help these girls
out. But I hope you learn from this.''

"She was really nice," Robyn would remember. "Possibly in shock. Or not really knowing what to say. I was
left with the feeling that she wasn't mad at us. Which is, I
think, what she was trying to say. That she wasn't mad at
us."

It would be the last time that anybody in Richmond saw
Cathy Wilson with a smile on her handsome, tanned face.
Certainly the truth of her loss had begun to sink in that first
week, but the rage that would propel her through the next
year—years, maybe—of her life had simply not surfaced
yet. Her behavior toward Dana spoke volumes about this
transformation; it turned 180 degrees after that visit to 210
South Belmont.

Perhaps, as Cathy began to learn the abhorrent details of
Stacey's murder, she realized that she wouldn't sleep until
somebody paid. Maybe it happened as she was planning
Stacey's funeral back in Lynchburg and putting together
photographs for the poster board that would be going on
display at the funeral home.

The service, which took place at night, was packed tight.
Some people were surprised to see that Stacey had so many
friends. A long stream of high-school buddies, restaurant co-
workers, and neighbors filed past her open casket to the tune
of "Tears in Heaven" by Eric Clapton and Puff Daddy's
"I'll Be Missing You."

In Richmond that August there was a memorial for Stacey
in the Metropolitan Community Church's stately white col-
umned building on the northern edge of the Fan. The very
same church where Turtle had schemed so recently about
her wedding with Tracy.

PART SIX

Glass Bricks

"Believe In Me," by Turtle Tibbs

I never meant her any harm
I was out of my head
I loved her with all my heart
and still can't believe she's dead.

When I realized what was happening
It was much too late
I wish I could turn back the hands of time
and change her fate.

She's gone home now
and will suffer no more
But I deal with guilt every day
and my heart is sore

I'm living in a cell
and I'm just a kid
Believe in me
Because no one ever did

26:

The women's wing of the Chesterfield County Jail is a cement loop of dormitories arranged around a busy little glass-bubble guardpost. The doors on the dorms are glass too, and these slide open and closed at the flip of a switch. When the lighting is right, it's a one-way view from inside the bubble: An inmate heading out to see a visitor encounters her own reflection and then the door clicks back into place behind her.

Prisoners pass their time at wooden picnic tables, some with their heads tilted back at an elevated television screen. Misdemeanors wear blue jumpsuits and felonies wear orange. Glass bricks in the dormitory roofs glow when it's sunny and fade to gray when it rains.

Sometimes in the overnight hours there's a rush of arrests, and four of the women's dorms fill up all the way: two to a bunk, 12 bunks to a dorm. In the morning, at eight, a guard throws down a pile of disposable razors and nail clippers, each marked with an inmate's name. Then it's "Winckler!" or "Tibbs!" and after a while they're collecting them again.

At nine, the cleaning-up part of the day is over and the television goes on.

It takes a lot to distract the prisoners from the daytime shows—a junkie going into withdrawal, for instance, throwing up and rolling around on the floor. The woman is shaking and in pain, and the others look on and some of them want to do something, but she won't let anybody touch her burning skin.

There are, however, long stretches of the afternoon when

the television screen is dark. Depending on the company, on the mix of personalities on a particular day of the week, there might be a 12-Step confessional or a game of Telephone: ''I went to the store on Saturday morning. . . .'' whispered into one woman's ear and then all around the room, up and down the bunks and along the picnic benches.

Bonding with your dormmates is tricky, though; the changeover is brisk at Chesterfield, which is designed as more of a holding cell for the county courthouse up the street than a long-term prison. Friendships and romances are short-lived here.

On the other hand, you think you've said goodbye forever to the vice charge on your top bunk and there she is in court with you a week later. And then carrying a dinner tray at another jail, updating you on developments back at Chesterfield, where you've each waited several times now for an escort up to see a judge.

GED class and Bible Study can make the time go more quickly at Chesterfield, but it means leaving the dorm and that's a ''two-deputy move'' for murder charges, requiring full shackles and the constant company of two guards. Nobody is exactly fighting to let accused killers wander around enjoying the perks. But then, Chesterfield doesn't get a lot of murderers on the women's side of the jail.

A Richmond squad car left Domica and Turtle at the Chesterfield jail's 1960s, Mayberry-style, brick façade on the Monday morning after their arrest, and they lingered at the booking desk in shackles. A loud woman in a brown shirt and green pants asked if they had any allergies, handed them rule books, and explained that they were on ''Keep Separates.''

''If y'all happen to see each other in the hallway, y'all cannot communicate whatsoever,'' she bellowed.

There were also Keep Separates on the other two—whom this lady now described as ''enemies'': Tracy, already locked up somewhere inside this grim, low-slung building, and Stephanie, still on her way from the police station across the street, and headed for "isolation."

Turtle's first trek through that mechanical pathway of sliding doors took all day. She answered questions and learned more jail vocabulary while secluded in a holding cell, only vaguely aware of the buzz catching on—not just in the outside world but down the hall in the women's dorms. Local TV stations broadcast the sullen faces of Stacey Hanna's confessed killers at midday and again on their evening shows, and inmates at the Chesterfield County Jail were as riveted as anyone by the "Lesbian Love Triangle" murder.

That evening, when the door to dorm number 10 let in a strapping young white girl with a black eye and a fresh orange jumpsuit, it didn't take much to figure out who she was.

"Oh shit!" somebody squealed. "Aren't you—?"

But it was with only the most genuine surprise that Turtle now saw that this was going to be her star turn. Crossing that dormitory with the heat of so many eyes on her skin, she was sick with fear—and yet also buoyed by the fear she could see in some of the faces around her. So this is what being a murderer felt like?

Never mind, for now, the righteous innocence that had motivated her every move in the last day and a half: the plea to Diane, the winding explanation to Detective Mormando.

Turtle responded to the lady who had squealed with the careful, practiced indifference of a teenager.

"Whatever," she said.

Turtle found her bunk, slipped a jail-issue pillowcase over her jail-issue pillow, and put her head down. She was trying to sleep when the room hissed to life around her with whispers; somebody was knocking on the wall.

"Yo, Turtle," one of her dormmates now told her. "That's probably for you, kid."

Turtle sat up and saw that everybody was watching a

raggedy slip of paper make its way into dorm 10 through
the tight space underneath a fire door. And then she followed its elaborate, hush-hush retrieval—just outside the
guard bubble's line of sight. The dorm phone was right by
the fire door, and the trick was to stand there with the receiver in your hand, chatting away, and get it with your foot.

This particular correspondence was for a "Tibbs."

Turtle flattened the note and leaned down into it. She
knew it: It was from Tracy.

"Don't turn on me," the love of her life had written.

What?

Turtle's new roommates looked on from a distance and
took in her baffled expression with the familiarity and interest of a sitcom audience. This relationship was simply
preceded by its reputation. And this murder was the most
interesting crime to concern the women's dorms for a while.

Turtle was perplexed by the workings of Tracy's mind.
Where were the love and kisses? What did she mean by
"Don't turn on me"? Which part of their long, bloody night
had she kept from the cops?

On the back of the same scrap, Turtle wrote, "I'm not
saying anything that didn't happen," and sent it back under
the door.

It turned out that Domica was in the next dorm—number
9—and Tracy, over in number 8 since before dawn, was on
Domica's other flank, mere feet away.

Tracy's proximity had its usual eerie effect on Turtle. She
was aware that night, in the minutes before she finally joined
the slow, measured breathing of the sleeping bodies around
her, of feeling better now. Her anger at Tracy—for not loving her enough, for being such a hothead—had already begun to drain away in that room at the police station. Now
it was almost gone.

She was stronger for Tracy wanting something from her,
and she was stronger for having Tracy on her side, not set
against her anymore in that horrible race not to tattle.

And it turned out that Turtle was not the only one feeling

empowered by this virtual reunion. As little as any of them wanted to revisit the three-headed monster they had become the other night, they had felt so much smaller ever since. This "Keep Separate" business allowed them their first righteous indignation since the one that had gotten them into trouble.

Here was a new unifying cause: It was unfair to put walls between them!

The next day, Domica passed ever-more urgent notes between dorms 8 and 10, giving them a close read of her own on the walk between fire doors. Meanwhile, the girls' irritation at being separated fed a steady stream of storytelling out loud to anyone in the Chesterfield County Jail dorms who would listen.

Turtle, Tracy, and Domica were much younger than most of the women in the jail they were talking to. Maybe that's what brought on the extra dose of bravado when answering questions or even just going about the business of making their beds or buttoning up their jumpsuits under the sometimes awestruck, sometimes hateful, but always curious glare of their dormmates.

Domica and Turtle also communicated in writing during those first days, passing their own notes under the door between 9 and 10. And at one point they were looking for someone to blame for their rather inevitable circumstance.

"Did they arrest Stephanie?" Domica wrote.

Turtle had heard that. "I think so."

"So it was probably her," Domica wrote back. Meaning that getting arrested last and then going into isolation was enough to clinch the theory that it was Stephanie who had called the cops in the first place. It made sense.

Tuesday stretched out in a blur of new faces, jail food, and mesmerizing television newscasts. It had started at a "popular drinking spot" in Chesterfield County; they were being charged with murder; they had not been remorseful when speaking to police. A Channel 8 camera panned the sodden forest off Nash Road.

Turtle's leg wound was infected by the time the jail infirmary took a look; it had to be cut open—drained not just of pus but of gravel and mud—and packed with gauze. It was too late for stitches.

Time was also running out on the chatty little circus in the women's dorms. Deputies at the jail put in calls to Detective Mormando to report that the Love Triangle girls were talking to each other a lot and telling everybody else about the murder too. When the detective himself came by to check it out, he got an earful of the same from some of the inmates.

The sheriff's department came up with a plan to get them through the month or two until their indictments: Domica and Turtle would stay at Chesterfield, divided by something more substantial than a fire door. On Wednesday morning, Stephanie would be ferried to Riverside Regional Jail, a sprawling new facility half an hour to the southeast. And Tracy would go back to Richmond.

They would spend their days and nights as far away from each other as possible. Until somebody could figure out just who was going to be menacing to whom—and who needed to be watched for more discreet influence.

27:

"She never said she was sorry for what she did. She just said, 'I hate fucking being here. I wanna get out.' She was very upset about being locked up. Not for the fact of what she did; that came out later: 'I wanna get out! Get—me—out!' "

—Sandy

When Tracy jingled into the Richmond City Jail that Wednesday, hunched forward and shuffling in her high-class, murderer-weight metal, she got looks there too. The celebrity of her case would make her some friends. In those first few days of captivity, though, it was allies on the outside that Tracy craved, even as she felt them slipping away.

Her mother showed up on her second day at Richmond, and through several layers of glass, Tracy could see what was happening.

Joanne Seward, a youthful, spare woman, had some of her daughter's height but an uprightness of posture that was all her own. This generally made her look proud, but today she was a picture of shame. She took a seat across from her daughter, now an imposing stranger with a peachfuzz head and a long, pumpkin-colored jumpsuit, and told her that she had broken her heart.

Tracy watched and listened to this distraught but solemn woman as if from a distance. She had felt her mother's disapproval for so long that it seemed natural. But what she was saying now was different: Tracy became convinced in this first jailhouse encounter of theirs that her mother didn't like her anymore.

When their time was up, Tracy returned to her bunk a zombie. A numbing inventory of her life confirmed that she had nothing now—except, maybe, for Sandy. And so she began right then, pen in hand, long feet over the end of the bed, to devote herself to the project of keeping her, the indecision of before now utterly gone in this vacuum.

Tracy failed, however, to guess what Sandy wanted to hear. In the days that followed, she plunged headlong not into regret but self-pity.

Her first, reluctant glimpses inside her own soul came as withdrawals from the pleasures of the physical world. She started to see that there might be no more driving around in her car for a while, no surfing in Hawaii, no T-ball with her little brother. Even sounds—like Sandy's favorite Mariah Carey song on the jail radio—could start off a torturous parade of images.

She remembered the "tingle" in her stomach when she and Sandy used to kiss, and tenderly described a lovemaking pose in one of her letters. Please send a picture, she urged, reminding Sandy of the words of a song they had liked by the Blessed Union of Soul: "You don't know what you have till your everything is gone."

After the first week, Sandy started dropping hints about breaking up. Tracy wrote that she understood: Sure, Sandy had to get on with her life out there. But mere paragraphs later, she hoped Sandy would be her "wife."

Tracy also wrote to Sandy that she sympathized with Stacey's mom and hoped that nothing like this would happen to her own kids, if she raised any. Which, well, she would very much like to do—with Sandy, she told her. Tracy sketched Sandy some yin/yang and peace symbols, a broken heart, and a drawing of herself as a karate blackbelt.

There were stray moments of mourning, genuine horror at what she had done, but in most of her letters, and in her conversations with Sandy on the phone and in visits to the jail, Tracy couldn't quite take responsibility for it.

Why, she asked rhetorically in one letter, did they go to the South Belmont Avenue house that Saturday night after the cookout? *Why?* That was the mistake, it seemed; that she had put herself in the path of a dangerous force—which had in turn caused this painful separation from Sandy.

But most important of all: Did Sandy know that Tracy wasn't a killer? That she would now give her own life to undo what had happened? Maybe she'd be out of jail in ten years, she suggested, begging Sandy to hold on, and not to hate her. In a sketch, a very short-haired jailbird standing behind bars spat an apology into a bubble.

Sandy wasn't convinced that Tracy understood what she had done and what it was going to mean. She told friends that she was scared of her and relieved that Tracy was behind bars now.

She was even more afraid of Turtle, though.

"What if I'da stayed that night?" Sandy asked Tracy once. "What if I'd been encouraged to go along on this little trip? Would y'all have done that to me?"

"Hell no!" Tracy balked.

"Tracy, what's the difference? If Turtle wanted to get rid of somebody who was trying to intervene between you and her, I was the girlfriend to you. What do you think she had in mind for me?"

Sandy was not the only one thinking along those lines, either. That first week after Tracy's arrest, Karla recalled a night she had spent at Turtle's place earlier that summer when Tracy was still living there officially.

"If you ever fucking think of going back out with Tracy," Turtle had joked, "I'll fucking kill you."

If Tracy's doubts about Sandy had faded with her own freedom, her feelings about Turtle were not so easily resolved. The whole Stacey thing had been Turtle's fault; her refusal that night to do her own dirty work was infuriating in retrospect. Now maybe Turtle was going to come out of this looking more innocent than Tracy. That was the "turning" of Tracy's first entreaty—and it remained one of her greatest fears. But Tracy still had some gummed-up feelings of love for Turtle too.

On Tracy's 20th birthday—August 3rd—Turtle wrote that she loved her. And Tracy said the same thing back.

Turtle also told her about Stacey's funeral back in Lynchburg. Dana had gone up there, she said, and seen Stacey laid out in a coffin under a heavy film of makeup. That was horrible enough, Turtle went on, but get this: Stacey's mom was threatening to kill all five of them—Dana was on her hit list too—if they showed up in Richmond again.

When Turtle professed her love in yet another letter, Tracy snarled to Sandy that if she truly cared, then Tracy wouldn't be in jail at all. She counted and compared her three broken hearts: Karla, who had hurt her so suddenly and deeply; Turtle, who just wasn't capable of loving her enough; and, well, Sandy was Tracy's *own* fault, she had to concede.

Karla, by now, could be trusted again. Or so Tracy thought. That first week, at the Richmond jail, Tracy placed a call to the twins. They were genuinely glad to hear from her.

"Oh, Tracy," Karla gushed, "how are you?"

She bitched a little about not making Tracy's three-person visitors' list, but in a friendly way—in a nervous way: Tracy didn't know yet that it was their father who had summoned the police.

28:

"When I got there first, I started hanging with Stephanie and Kelley. And different people come up to me like, 'You better watch out 'cause you know what they're in here for.' And I'm like, 'No, not really.' And they were like, 'Them's the girls that murdered that girl.' And then I recognized their faces.

"So the next time I went in there was two or three weekends later. They put me in the cell with Tracy. She would holler over for Kelley so I got to kinda figure out who she was. So I started talkin' to her, and I asked her, 'Why y'all do that? Why did y'all go and beat up that girl?' And she says she didn't really think something like that was gonna happen.

"And I asked Stephanie that too. You know, 'Why y'all do that? Who did what?' 'Cause I was curious. And she's like, 'Let me ask you something, sister.' She said, 'Do you think we deserve to die?' I said, 'You know what, Stephanie? I'm going to tell you like this.' I say, 'Y'all deserve to get what y'all deserve to get,' I said, 'because there was no reason for that girl to die like that.'

"She had just got done telling me about her childhood and I didn't mean to come off like that. But she looked at me and she was like, 'You just struck my feelings.' And she started crying. And then I got kicked out of the gym and I wasn't allowed back in the gym.

"And then when I got a chance to talk to Domica, she was just nonchalant and blunt. Like 'Okay I did this. I'm scared, but—' You know how different people are. 'I'm sorry for what I did, but ain't nothing I can do.' She just told me that she regrets ever hanging out with them.

"If you didn't know what they did, you wouldn't be able to tell that they would ever do something like that. Because they were sweet people. You know, some people you can hang around and like, man, that's a bad influence."

—Crystal Robinson, 20, weekend inmate at Riverside Regional Jail, September 1997–January 1998

Riverside Regional Jail, which had opened just 15 days before Stacey Hanna's murder, is neither a cramped, county brig like Chesterfield nor an urban dungeon like the Richmond City Jail. Bright turquoise panels accent a maze of long, windowless hallways and pre-poured concrete octagons, and the careful design seems to suit the modern approach to jailing that inspires the place: We will regulate your every move, but you will always have something to do.

Riverside rises unremarkably like a cluster of college dorms from a dusty plain just over Chesterfield County's southeastern border. At first glance, from the narrow country road that shoots up at it from the highway, the jail might be employee housing for the much more imposing federal men's prison next door.

The simplicity is an illusion, though. Riverside was put up with great forethought during a period of frantic jail-building around the state. Seven southeastern Virginia jurisdictions send in prisoners under special service agreements.

For five of the seven, Riverside is the local jail, and squad cars ferry their arrests in directly from a network of local police stations. The other two, Chesterfield County and the city of Petersburg, pass on the overflow from existing jails, especially any inmates expecting long trials. Murder trials, for instance.

Riverside prisoners—there were upwards of 700 in its first year of operation—live in "pods." A pod is two curved tiers of individual cells wrapped around one side of an open "common area," with tables for eating anchored to a raised platform at the inside of the arc.

Jail administrators emphasize that they can move their charges around on a moment's notice, but that debut year, at least, women lived in Pods A and B, with a 12-bed quadrant of Pod C set aside for Keep Separate cases, "disciplinary" problems, and certain high-security prisoners on their way in from the outside.

You get your own cell in B or share one in A, behind a genuine door on hinges. Each has a toilet, a sink, a desk, a mirror, and a window out to the grassy grounds.

The rules—such as no physical contact between cellmates and no tipping photographs against the wall behind your desk—are harder to enforce when the door is closed: during lockdowns at noon, 6 p.m., and bedtime, for example. But guards walk by at intervals and you can hear them coming, barking out a count or making an announcement. A narrow strip of glass in the door fills with a deputy's face if there's something she wants to see.

Inmates also spend hours a day in the open space between buildings, a concrete yard with a basketball court under a neat square of sky. Plus there's weightlifting once a week in the gym, Life Skills, Narcotics Anonymous, Alcoholics Anonymous, and GED.

For clothes, it's jailwear or nothing at Riverside, unless you have the cash "on your books" to pick up a Hanes t-shirt or a pair of blue gym shorts from the canteen. The standard teal-green jumpsuit—never, ever to be worn unbuttoned—is only required for recreation and visitors.

The lone exception to the ban on personal style is shoes, a small detail that emphasizes sneaker choice way beyond the proportions even of the average high school.

The rules about getting shoes in from the outside seemed to change with the seasons that first trial-and-error year, but mostly you were stuck with what you walked in on. Or a pair of the canteen Reeboks. There were rumors all the time that they would also be getting Nikes in.

Stephanie was the first to arrive at Riverside. She spent five weeks as the sole representative of the Lesbian Love Triangle Murder. Her mother was relieved at first that she got the modern jail, figuring that modern medicine would be part of the deal. But right away, Stephanie's health took a turn for the worse; some mornings she couldn't move her legs enough to get across her cell to the toilet.

She was getting the right arthritis medicine—antimalaria pills, steroids, and nonsteroidal antiinflammatory drugs— but Cindy complained that the jail doctor didn't see her enough to monitor side effects.

And then one day, Stephanie stumbled to the mirror over her sink and saw that her hair was growing in snow-white. At first the streaks were just pencil-thin, but these quickly widened into stripes. Doctors' best guess was an overdose of antimalaria pills, and the dosage was adjusted. But Stephanie's hair continued to whiten—with eerie effect: Her adult predicament was already so out of character for one so slow in growing up, and now her body was racing ahead at breakneck speed as well.

A good shrink might have been more help to Stephanie even than steady attention to the mix of her arthritis drugs. Every night when she settled into bed, she was back at that dark road again or staring into Stacey's bloodied face. Sedatives got her through the worst times, but now she was sleeping too much and getting fat and depressed.

And then in early September, one of her nightmares came true: "I'm bringing Tibbs in here with you," a lieutenant told her.

To Riverside? To A Pod?

Word traveled quickly on the network of prisoners shuttled back and forth between Riverside and Chesterfield, or waiting together in courthouse holding cells. By now, everybody knew: Capital murder charges—death penalty charges—

were being considered only for the other three. And they were mad that Stephanie was getting off easy. The favorite theory being that this was in reward for snitching.

It was too much: Vicious behavior had put Stephanie in jail, and yet her once good friends found her not vicious enough.

Either way, it was the usual problem. Floating, directionless, Stephanie had opted the night of the murder not to risk disapproval and find herself alone. And look where it had gotten her. Stephanie had never felt so alone in her life.

As it turned out, Turtle arrived back in Stephanie's life without a great deal of fuss. She was friendly—and full of other concerns.

"Do you have any pictures of Stacey?" she asked Dana over an A Pod telephone on one of her first days at Riverside.

"No, I don't," came the answer. "But if I find any I'll mail some in to you."

That was Turtle's refrain; she asked everyone on the outside the same question. Sometimes she was told there were no photographs just handy; sometimes the person on the other end of the line simply found it too strange a request and hoped Turtle would get over it.

"All right, that's cool," she would say, "because I don't know if I can deal with it either."

Then one day Turtle got a package in the mail, an envelope with no return address. There was another envelope inside that one and then a photograph of Stacey. But no note, no name.

Nope, Dana told her on the phone, she hadn't sent it.

A letter followed in a matter of days, saying something like this:

"Don't ever think you're going to walk out those doors. Because as soon as you do, you're going to be buried six feet. You're going to walk right into a grave and be buried six feet."

Just as upsetting for Turtle, however, was the deafening

silence at ROSMY since her arrest. She wrote them a letter, wondering, "How can you call yourself a support group? You're not going to give it to us because we made one mistake?" Executive Director Chris Clarke wrote back and tried to explain that the case could do the group harm, that reaching out to the girls would made it look like ROSMY was supporting what they had done.

Turtle was relieved when Jon Klein came to Riverside on a sneak visit, but she stayed mad at ROSMY. And Diane. And all the other old friends who had cut her off. Couldn't they see that she was still the same old Turtle underneath?

29:

Domica was already at the courthouse in a basement holding cell of her own when Stephanie and Turtle were escorted in on September 15th. The other two were separated from Domica—and from the citizens and lawyers and evidence closets and libraries upstairs—by a grid of old-fashioned steel bars. They all reclined on metal benches.

Tracy, stiff and scowling, marched in last. When an officer put her down across from Stephanie and Turtle, her expression, as Turtle would describe it later, said, "All of you are shit."

The occasion that now put the four of them within the sound of each other's voices for the first time in the six weeks since their arrests was a joint preliminary hearing, a chance for Chesterfield County District Court Judge Philip Daffron to see if the Commonwealth had solid cases here. Maybe they would also be indicted today.

"Oh my God," Turtle told Tracy right off. "I can't believe I've been away from you this long."

Tracy looked up, looked down again.

"Are you gonna talk to me or what?" Turtle asked.

"I don't know, Turtle."

"What do you mean you don't know? You fucked my life up and you don't know if you're gonna talk to me?"

That got her attention.

"You fucked *my* life up! I did this shit for *you*!"

"No, you didn't!"

Domica piped up just then from the other cell.

"Shut the fuck up, y'all. We're not supposed to talk about this bullshit."

Turtle leaned forward and spoke quietly. She was almost whispering.

"Are you gonna talk to me?"

Several more minutes passed. Turtle leaned back against the wall of the cell and looked up at the ceiling.

"I miss you so much," she said.

"Yeah."

"I love you."

Tracy considered that for a few seconds. Less time than Turtle expected.

"Me too," Tracy said.

It was like ice melting; the distance of these six weeks took several more minutes to fully thaw. But then it did. And they kissed.

"I could spend the rest of my life in this one little cell with you and I'd be all right, because I had you," Turtle told her.

Leaving that holding cell was hard enough without facing a courtroom lined with family members and the cold, hard recollections of the police. The cinder block, the boxcutters, the cruel encounters at that open trunk—the details of their night with Stacey were laid out for the first time in plain sight of the world, of Judge Daffron, of everybody's parents.

"They left her, went down the road, talked about how Stacey could identify them and potentially put them in jail, or get them in trouble," Detective Zeheb recalled of his conversation with Tracy, summarizing briskly.

Then, he said, "They had talked about how they needed to kill her.

"They turned around, went back, picked up Stacey, put her in the trunk of the vehicle, and drove around with her, for what Tracy Bitner indicated was at least 45 minutes. Took her to Nash Road. Got her out of the trunk of the vehicle. Walked her down the road to the site where her body was found, and cut her and beat her some more."

Detective Zeheb said he saw few signs of regret in the behavior of his charge, and Detective Mormando said the same about Domica—who at times seemed, along with Turtle, to be motivated by the pettiest concerns.

"She admitted that she and Kelley Tibbs kicked the victim down, forcing the victim's face to go down into the mud—because they got mud all over their shoes," Detective Mormando told the court.

Turtle's lawyer waived a public examination of her confession so as not to overly titillate the press, but he did want to know how close that big stick had been to the body when Detective Zeheb came upon it. The detective's answer was "very close."

Tracy, Turtle, and Domica were indicted that afternoon on charges of robbery, abduction—and because of the robbery, capital murder. They would be going to trial sometime in the winter.

And although their lawyers were there chirping "Don't worry"-s and smiling with the various mothers, the facts spoke for themselves: A guilty verdict on a capital murder charge was going to mean lethal injection or life in jail. *Life* in jail, there being no parole in Virginia for violent crimes.

Stephanie's case was remanded to a later session—another suspicious turn, in the eyes of the other three. In fact, Judge Daffron only granted the delay because Stephanie's lawyer hadn't received a promised transcript of her confession, and because there was still no autopsy report. The rumors had been right, though: She was indicted for first-degree murder seven weeks later in November, a charge for which the penalty is 20 years to life.

30:

"You don't own me, muthafucka!"

"You didn't bring this TV wich you to jail when you came, bitch!"

Fights at Riverside could be loud. A good couple of shrieks in the cavernous common area were enough to drown out even the steady slip-slap of cards going down on tabletops. Arguments about television channels—Was it going to be Ricky Lake or Jerry Springer?—had been known to spill blood.

More serious altercations, on the other hand, tended to creep up unseen and unheard—and to have been dragged in from the outside world from rivalries, love affairs, and crimes past.

In late September, when Tracy and Domica joined the other two down at Riverside, the main concern was about testimony being sweet-talked or terrorized into changing before the lawyers got the chance to play out their various strategies in court.

And so, in the months to come, they were never more than two to a pod. Stephanie could be with Turtle or Tracy, that was all. It seems the only instructions were to keep Domica alone and the infamous ex-lovers apart.

Domica had herself requested Keep Separates on all three the moment she got to Riverside, and very soon she stopped answering mail. Her role as the annoyed one, above the petty emotional fray of the sweethearts and the tattletale, turned into something much more mysterious and invisible.

The calm she had shown in the face of Stacey's death,

the matter-of-factness that had repulsed readers of the Richmond *Times–Dispatch*, had tended to soothe her jittery accomplices. Now she was simply out of touch.

This was partly indignation that the others had mentioned the watch—she was especially angry with Turtle, the first to bring it up with Detective Mormando that night at the Richmond police station. As fall turned to winter, it became clear that Domica's case hinged very directly on that small, innocuous item. That and the rings she had taken from Stacey, although the police had still not found those.

But there was more to her silence than that. Just as before that last Sunday in July, Domica's tough-guy talk, her menacing "Don't make me beat your ass," had been mistaken so often for the repartee of an experienced fighter, now people tended not to see that Domica was deeply depressed.

Like Stephanie, she had the tendency even before the murder to fall into dark, suicidal moods; unlike Stephanie, she had never developed the ability to communicate about it. They all got threats in the mail—even Dana, who began staying away from visiting hours at Riverside because of them and eventually quit her job to go into hiding at her parents' house in nearby Colonial Heights. But Domica took everything to heart.

At one point, her dreams got so bad at night that she slept during the day instead. She dreamt about Stacey looking at her through the little square window in her cell, then that she had been the one killed instead, and later that it was her own mother.

For Domica, this thing that had happened to her—this thing that she had done on Turtle's behalf, pretty much— was just the worst in a long string of letdowns. Certainly she figured it wasn't the last.

One day, she got a surprise visit from her father. Her mom had been by, and her grandfather, and some of the others—but Michael Davis? She wasn't expecting it.

The visiting areas at Riverside are long, boxy rooms with stools attached to the floor alongside a wall of thick, steel-bolted windows. The only way to get close is to sit all the

way up inside one of the deep, flat window sills that angle
out at about thigh height. The guards discourage this.

Not to worry. That kind of whispery, cuddly communi-
caton was not what Domica or her father had in mind. Their
conversation was strained and brief. But Michael came back
a second time and even left Domica with some money and
his telephone number.

It was a good deal more than he'd given her in a while—
and there was hell to pay. His wife Bonnie kicked him out
of the house until he finally promised not to go back to the
jail.

Separate meant just that at Riverside. There was no stealth
note-passing under Riverside's long, solid doors. Anything
on paper went through the mail, all the way out to the U.S.
Postal Service and back again. As a fortress of microman-
agement, Riverside lived up to its reputation.

Of course there were gaps—quirks, really, more than
failures in the machine—that permitted stray moments of
communication. When A Pod was in the yard, B Pod could
send big-lunged greetings through the grates that ringed the
outer wall there, above eye level. And sometimes A and B
overlapped on basketball breaks.

Turtle and Tracy also used two more quiet venues: the
library, where whispers over an open law book generally
went unnoticed—and church.

Church services were a weekly event open to both pods,
and they were held in the gym, where the bare walls and
floor bounced every musical note and human breath into a
cacophonous blur. You carried a stool in from your pod and
put it down where you liked. It was no trouble at all getting
in a discreet conversation when the choir was shouting out
a hymn or the minister delivering a sermon.

It was at one such moment that Tracy leaned over and
told Turtle that the twins' father, Wayne Felice, was the one
who had called the police; the girls had admitted it just the
other day during visiting hours.

Turtle had long ago dropped her suspicions of Stephanie,

who was still her podmate when this latest news came down. But Tracy?

"Why the fuck did you tell?" Turtle demanded.

"I didn't tell anybody but Karla and Danielle."

"What the fuck? Didn't we just say, 'This won't leave the car'?"

"I just needed to tell somebody."

"But Karla and Danielle? Couldn't you just randomly go to a bum on the street? Couldn't you hold it all in, write it down, talk to me?"

Turtle loved moments such as this when Tracy was pushed into the penitent role. Turtle was supposed to be the wild, out-of-control one, but look at whose friend spilled the beans. The fact that Turtle herself had run just as quickly to Diane's was beside the point.

This would seem less and less important later on. Right now, it was a matter of pride between Turtle and Tracy, still watching the balance shift every day between their mutual blame and affection. Indulging the crushes around them and spending time working out at the gym only went so far to distract them from this game.

Most everyone was glad when they finally got new girl-friends.

Tracy hooked up with a girl named Dawn; "Truly, Madly, Deeply" by Savage Garden was their song. And Turtle started "seeing" Courtney—a good choice during chance moments of intimacy because Courtney didn't register on the guards' couple radar; they all seemed to think she was straight.

Stephanie was the very youngest inmate at Riverside in those first months and perhaps the most childlike. There were advantages to that. She could always—always—count on the mothering of her podmates, which in jail translates not just into friends but protection too.

Riverside wasn't the battleground of an overcrowded men's prison, but some women were simply on top—and not prepared for changes on the totem pole. Once, at a card game, Stephanie got tired of playing and threw her cards down. The gesture was considered unacceptable: An older woman with a good hand who was counting on winning smacked her around to teach her a lesson about disrespect.

Lucky for Stephanie that she also had younger girls for friends, like Chrissy, who didn't play power games and didn't run the other way fast on Stephanie's darker, withdrawn days. And Claire, who was slowly becoming Stephanie's "girlfriend" again, jail or no jail. Claire visited every week and stood by at home after work to accept collect calls. They liked to think of their renewed connection as some kind of rough diamond that this earthquake had knocked loose from stone—and yet placed out of reach.

"It was like, 'Hello! This is what you've been missing out on,' " Claire would say. "Now it's too late. There's nothing you can do about it."

The tragedy worked for both of them, though, and met not entirely unfamiliar needs: Stephanie enjoyed Claire's connection to reality, and Claire had Stephanie where she could finally have some semblance of control.

As jailbirds, Turtle, Tracy, Domica, and Stephanie were pretty much the same people they had been on the outside, getting around "pod" society with the same extremes of initiative and helplessness that had gotten them that far.

With more time alone, they were also clearer and clearer about what kind of young women they were not: None believed herself capable of committing murder on her own.

It was in part for that reason that the camaraderie that had flourished between them immediately after their arrests turned steadily to resentment. The longer each stayed in jail, the surer she was about it: She wouldn't be there if it weren't for "the others."

This way of thinking played nicely into their lawyers' plans for court—indeed, some of them were actively behind it. But it also stunted the girls' chances of understanding Stacey's death, not to mention the wisdom of "kicking ass" as the best method of punishment.

Some families were less helpful than others in helping the girls look at where exactly they had gone wrong.

Tracy's step-dad wrote her a letter saying how very disappointed he was in her, and how all this lesbian stuff had affected him and his friends. If only she'd managed to keep away from lesbians, he seemed to be saying, then none of this would have happened.

31:

Robyn came down from Dale City on New Year's Eve and stopped into Babe's for a dose of lesbian culture. It was a cold and unsettling experience. People she knew from a distance—"nice to see you" kind of friends—didn't even have that to say. She'd glance up from her bottle of Icehouse and they'd be shooting her dirty looks.

Robyn wondered, How long till everyone stopped seeing her and thinking *murder*? She felt branded by this thing—or maybe it was her continued connection to Turtle.

No, Robyn and Richmond weren't ready for each other yet. She put in a visit to Turtle down at Riverside and headed back up north.

Marsh Field also gained a certain notoriety after the murder, some of it for the good. There was less 3 a.m. traffic for a while, and a long, refreshing absence of beer cans and spray paint. The only real surprise was the free advertising that Stacey Hanna generated for Walter Marsh's pilots' club.

Marsh Field's immortalization in the press as "a popular drinking spot" had stuck. The television reporters had picked it up from the *Richmond Times–Dispatch*, and then *The Washington Post* had taken it national. Another proprietor of another piece of trespassed, bloodied land might have minded, but here was a man with a drinking club and a sense of humor. Walter Marsh took it as a cute, if ineffectual, little boost for his Tuesday night parties.

He had tried to clean the vandals' paint from the "Marsh Field" sign on his white picket fence down at the road, but the green backing kept coming off along with the paint. And so, one day that winter he had a new one made up—with that extra phrase across the middle. The sign now read "Marsh Field, a popular drinking spot," with the address down at the bottom.

"It's sorta like you get a plug in the newspaper for a restaurant," was his explanation.

A few miles away, at the other end of Stacey's bumpy, airless ride, where she had last left Stephanie and Dana in the car and headed out into the dark, another commemorative announcement went up that winter. Cathy Wilson fashioned a cross from two long white pieces of plywood and lettered the horizontal piece with her daughter's name and the other with the date of her birth—3/29/79—and death—7/27/97.

She secured this shoulder-high marker in the dirt between the pipe gate and the road, but over to the left a little so as not to be disturbed.

It was easy to miss if you came at it from the north, hidden as it was behind that fringe of trees. For drivers going the other direction, though, past the ever more advanced earth-moving at The Highlands, the cross was easily visible. At night it was an ominous white flash in the headlights of cars proceeding along Nash Road.

PART SEVEN

The Fence that Hemmed in the Terror

He ran stumbling through the thick sand to the open space of rock beyond the fire. Between the flashes of lightning the air was dark and terrible; and the boys followed him, clamorously. Roger became the pig, grunting and charging at Jack, who side-stepped. The hunters took their spears, the cooks took spits, and the rest clubs of firewood. A circling movement developed and a chant. While Roger mimed the terror of the pig, the littluns ran and jumped on the outside of the circle. Piggy and Ralph, under the threat of the sky, found themselves eager to take a place in this demented but partly secure society. They were glad to touch the brown backs of the fence that hemmed in the terror and made it governable.

"Kill the beast! Cut his throat! Spill his blood!"

—from Lord of the Flies, *by William Golding*

32:

The Stacey Hanna murder trials were more of an eye-opener for Chesterfield County than some of the area's more traditional Baptist preachers would like to admit. Never mind those first six cautionary months of seeing "lesbians" printed only next to "killers" in the news; now readers would come to know the mothers, the confused and quite average friends—and the innocent, infatuated victim herself. The surprise was less in hearing about "butches" or "dykes" for the first time than in recognizing that some of the basic rivalries behind this otherwise unimaginable incident were not so unlike one's own.

This is not to say that the county wasn't looking for a show: There was bound to be an embarrassing spectacle or two when the Lesbian Love Triangle girls went to trial—an angry mob at least.

Even more dramatic, the Commonwealth of Virginia might line up all three death penalty candidates at the same time—a despondent, forcibly groomed bunch in a tight row of chairs along one side of the courtroom. Commonwealth attorneys in tasseled loafers would march back and forth in front of them like righteous parents, openly contrasting the various blows to Stacey's body, the defendants' whimpering grudges against her, the boasting and lies at the end.

Group trials were an option in the Virginia law books at the time but very new: A 1993 statute broke an old tradition of trying co-defendants separately, bringing Virginia more in line with other states and the federal system.

Prosecutors who had done a lot of group trials usually liked them better. They welcomed juries' difficulty with the "hearsay" rules, which say that one defendant's statements about her own guilt can't be used against another. Jurors were told, *Remember this part but ignore that part*. And, in the confusion, they usually went ahead and sent the whole crew upriver.

But the County's team didn't have direct experience with that, and so their thinking was different in the Stacey Hanna case. They pictured six or so defense lawyers crammed into a single courtroom and popping up every few minutes like so many jacks-in-the-box. The objections would come one-by-one in an annoying slew of complaints about one client being "tainted" by another's gruesome behavior, or another being unfairly maligned by hearsay. Not very much of the Commonwealth's evidence would make it out to the jury room. And the chances of an appeal would be immense. Overturn one sentence and there, maybe, go all the rest.

The County Commonwealth Attorney's Office cherished its death penalty convictions too much to take the risk; there was the statewide record of Warren Von Schuch, the team's capital pointman, to defend. He had eleven men on death row just then.

No, the girls accused in the Stacey Hanna case would go one each before the four judges of the Chesterfield County Circuit Court in a long, repetitive gush of testimony that would last all winter. They would arrive in court humbled by isolation from each other and just vaguely aware of what had come before—like the media-saturated jurors who would linger at the photographs of the girls' handiwork and then finally remember each from the cast of characters they knew on television: the tall one, the short one, the black one, and the disabled one.

Of course, what close readers of the news knew even better than their looks were the actual roles the four were supposed to have played on the night of the murder. Until Domica Winckler went to trial just after New Year's, those had seemed the only relevant differences between them.

33:

"And you wonder why black folks don't trust the criminal justice system. We recently witnessed an outpouring of support for Karla Faye Tucker, a white female pickaxe murderer turned Christian who, despite the best efforts of the Rev. Pat Robertson, was executed Tuesday . . . We also read in the *Times–Dispatch* how Danville has sent more people to death row per capita than any other Virginia city. All of these condemned men happen to be African-American, even though whites commit a quarter of Danville's homicides. And now, we have the contrast between the trials of Tracy Lynn Bitner and Domica Winckler . . .

"Would Robertson have felt as strongly about Tucker's case if she had found, say, Allah instead of Jesus? What about rehabilitated atheists? And how would Robertson and Tucker's other supporters have responded if Tucker was black, like Winckler, or a lesbian?"

—Michael Paul Williams, columnist, *Richmond Times–Dispatch*, February 9, 1998

THE NEIGHBOR

Pleading not guilty was almost a formality in the three capital cases, a rational reflex in the face of the death penalty. They were all quite guilty of something—and Domica in almost all the wrong ways.

By the time she went to court in January, there was an

autopsy report showing two official causes of death, insanguination and drowning, and Domica could be directly linked to both. The holes she had punched in the flesh around Stacey's upper rib cage were not the only ones to bleed, for example, but she had punched so many of them. Enough on their own, it could be argued, to force Stacey into shock and prevent her from rescuing herself from the water around her.

Greg Carr, one of Domica's court-appointed attorneys, gave away the level of desperation on his side of the room during his opening statement, when he suggested that somebody had actually placed the boxcutter in her pocket. That was simply no match for the harder facts, or the eyewitness account of Domica's former friend, Dana Vaughan.

Dana was among the first to come to the stand, and she described the scene with the cinder block by the picnic table at Marsh Field, sweaty and blinking through her glasses as if Stacey were expiring again there before her in the courtroom. Even as her first-hand testimony faded to a soundtrack and panned away from Domica to the whole group, it was chilling.

"I saw shadows down the road," she said, "and I could only hear the footsteps after that. About a few minutes later, I heard a scream and it got muffled. And then I heard another scream, and then I heard it get muffled again. And that was it."

Some of the jurors cried when a bailiff passed around a startling set of 24-by-36-inch photographs of Stacey's mutilated body, and the Commonwealth conducted a long, dry back-and-forth with the attending cops about some tiny bags of hair and rings—not the stolen rings, which were still missing, but the as-yet-unidentified rings found on the ground at Marsh Field. Then came Domica's own damning videotaped descriptions and those cynical statements at the end.

The defendant's stiff, expressionless appearance in court seemed to fit just right after that. She was nothing like her mean, swollen mugshot, being greatly reduced in size, longer-haired, and dressed in a navy blue pantsuit and white blouse. But there was rarely even a twitch of recognition about what was going on here.

Capital murder has specific requirements, though, and neither the brutality of a killing nor a defendant's absence of regret necessarily figure. It was arguable that Domica should not be convicted of capital murder, as Virginia statutes describe it, but rather murder in the first degree—with a sentence of 20 years to life.

The Commonwealth insisted that the robbery made this a capital crime, and noted that while there were doubts about blaming Tracy, Turtle, and Stephanie for their victim's reduction that night to a tiny string anklet and those red underpants, Domica had confessed to taking the watch. But most readings of Virginia law insist on a "causal connection" between robbing a capital victim and killing her, and there was not a shred of evidence in the Commonwealth's case that Stacey had been murdered for her belongings.

"But my God, a watch is the turning point in the death penalty and life behind bars," Cary Bowen, Domica's other attorney, mused to the jury. "It's so small. It's so juvenile . . . Should that watch dictate death? . . . This is impulsive. This is spontaneous."

Even Tracy testified, weeping, to the unimportance of the watch, the rings, those clothes.

But it was all to no good. Judge Herbert Gill, Jr., sent the jury off to their deliberations without insisting on the "causal connection." And Domica was convicted of capital murder, abduction, and robbery—a crumpled, childlike figure with her head on the counsel table, now jittery with sobs, her first actual movement in days.

The sentencing phase of this first trial featured the mothers and friends of first Stacey and then Domica competing for the jury's sympathy, and what they had to say was not just sad but eerie: They laid out two almost parallel young lives, from the girls' Virginia births just five weeks apart in the late winter of 1979 to suicide attempts at 13. The hope was that one girl's pain would be conjured more sharply, enough to steer 12 Chesterfield County citizens between the two lone "recommendations" allowed: life in prison without parole or death by lethal injection.

At this point, it wasn't of any direct use to discuss alternative punishments, but Frank Winckler, Sr., Domica's grandfather, raised the question nonetheless. A small man with a white moustache and a flat, reassuring voice, when he spoke it was the first look at the big picture: the scourge of teen violence that would not truly be touched by any of the sentences on the table today.

He said he used to see Domica every week, even though he lived in the East End and she in the western part of the city. And they were very close. But instead of asking for forgiveness or understanding, he asked that Stacey's killers be put hard to work on the prevention end of this scourge.

"This is very painful," he said. "And I realize that what my granddaughter did is very serious. But I don't think taking another life is going to help this case or bring anyone back or help any young people in the future.

"I would like to see these young kids involved, make some videos and [sent] to schools and all other places, pleading with other kids not to do these type of things. Because I think they could reach them better than we can or the courts can or anybody. And I think this would be better punishment and a better solution than taking another life."

The jurors got up soon after Frank had returned to his seat. And two hours later, they returned a sentence of death—pending Judge Gill's approval at a separate session, scheduled three months of Riverside jail-time later, an imprimatur that all such cases require.

The uncertain status of this recommendation barely tempered the horror around the courtroom, though, as Domica's family wept and cried out. It was difficult not to make comparisons between 18-year-old Domica and the only woman ever put to death in Virginia history: a poor, black laundress in Elizabeth City County named Virginia Christian, who had been fighting with her white employer over a stolen shirt when the older lady dropped dead. She had just turned 17 when she died in the electric chair in 1912.

THE GIRLFRIEND

Tracy's trial in February, in the second of the Circuit Court's four matching beige courtrooms, was expected to be the same kind of shoo-in. It was under Tracy's oppressive arm, after all, that a miserable, pleading Stacey had been forced down that logging trail. And Tracy had confessed to cutting her throat, as vivid and treacherous an act as any. The swipe of her boxcutter had not severed a carotid artery—these run along either side of the neck; opening one of them would have killed Stacey in minutes. But the blade had cut her windpipe, helping to force water into her lungs.

The Commonwealth also figured that Tracy's mere size would work against her, perhaps even forcing that last leap of imagination that most people need to believe a woman capable of extreme violence.

Of course, convicting Tracy on capital murder also required a robbery. "Accessory" to robbery is a fuzzy area of the law, but getaway-car drivers do sometimes get the same punishment as the guy actually standing over the 7-Eleven cash drawer with a gun.

Domica herself came to court for Tracy's trial and testified to several incriminating details; she remembered hearing Tracy say, "We gotta kill her," for example. But Domica also said that taking the watch had been her decision alone; Tracy had had nothing to do with it.

"When you took the watch from her, that was an impulse you had; isn't that correct?" John Boatwright, Tracy's attorney, asked Domica. And she told him Yes.

In the end, Tracy Bitner didn't have to wait for the sentencing phase of her trial to know that she wouldn't be put to death. Judge F. John Daffron, Jr., said that to convict Tracy of capital murder, the robbery had to be "one of the motivating factors" for killing Stacey. And the jury dropped the charge to first-degree murder, along with robbery and abduction.

So it was with a different sense of her own destiny than she may have expected that Tracy stood tall on the last day of her trial and delivered a pre-prepared apology. Towering there in a brown v-neck sweater and khakis, she wasn't asking for her life after all, but to be able to leave jail at middle age.

Tracy's chestnut hair had grown out a little since the videotaped confession that the jury had watched earlier, and it waved slightly. But the same emotional turmoil was there in her face and words, and it poured out again in a mix of self-doubt and undirected despair. She paused sometimes to keep from crying.

"This is to the judge, the jury, and the people," she started.

"Somebody asked me, 'How could you do that? Only God is supposed to take a life.' I answered that question with a shrug of my shoulder and a tear from my eye. My life has just begun because another has ended. I have no answers for the questions being asked. I'm still looking for them for myself and her mother.

"On the night of July 27th, a life was taken. A part of me died as I made a choice of my life, the choice that I cannot change but would give my life to do so. I've made a horrible mistake that now I have to live with. The worst punishment is my memory of that night, a night I will never be able to forget.

"People have told me to ask for forgiveness. Well, I can't. I can't forgive myself, much less to ask God to forgive me. I have so many feelings inside of me that I don't know how to express, some as to my family, mostly my mother. I've let her down in the biggest way. It will never be the same between us.

"I love her so much, and this is not the way to show her. Saying I'm sorry from the bottom of my heart is what I'm trying to say. No. Sorry doesn't make it okay or even let it go away. It's staying.

"I'm saying I'm truly sorry for the mistake I made. I deserve not to be forgiven but only wish to be heard. I owe my life to her mother, the mother that loved her child more than anything for anything. I wish I could take all her pain away that I've caused. No, I do not pray, but I will today. I will pray not for myself but for you to be okay."

The jury recommended two life terms plus ten years, and that was harsh. But the contrast with Domica's predicament was shocking. Was it Domica's more direct connection to that watch that had brought on the death sentence? Was it her unfeeling demeanor? Had the instructions given Tracy's jury made the difference? Or was it that one girl was black and the other white?

Anybody watching the clouds gather behind Domica's eyes that winter guessed that she might have preferred the death penalty over 40 years in a penitentiary, but that was hardly the point. The history of racial unevenness on death row was easily summoned—in newspaper columns, at church meetings, and over kitchen counters. Relations between black and white were about to suffer badly in the Richmond area if these sentences were carried out.

Many Virginians didn't see Domica's sentence as racist, though—and it wasn't just the rednecks. While there was only one black juror at Domica's trial, some people pointed out, there were only two at Bitner's. And whatever the peculiar legal wrinkles about the others being "accessories" to the robbery, Domica's jurors might have been justified in punishing the actual thief.

THE DRIVER

The matter of that yawning gap between the first two sentences was far from settled when Stephanie limped into the courtroom at the end of March for her own reckoning. The thought was that this third trial could not possibly cause such a controversy, not being about capital murder.

But Stephanie's trial was, in fact, the most openly contentious so far.

For starters, the Commonwealth lawyers weren't happy with her fancy lawyer's famous harping: Every one of Joe Morrissey's objections seemed to lead to another lengthy sidebar or another tug of war about showing this photograph or that one.

The Commonwealth was also disappointed with Claire Watson for failing to recall some key memories until she got up there on the stand. She was supposed to be a prosecution witness just then—although a defense witness later in the trial—and yet she was going on and on in Mr. Morrissey's cross-examination about how scared poor Stephanie had been of Turtle that Sunday afternoon on the phone.

This was the crux of Stephanie's defense: that her passive-aggressive behavior was explained by pure fear. It was a stretch, given the evidence. She hadn't been at the actual murder scene, but neither had she driven away or pulled her car up as it bypassed the Chesterfield County police station between assaults—with Stacey in the trunk. Stephanie had also not resisted inflicting some pain of her own.

But Morrissey described Stephanie as a handmaiden among thugs. For days, the jury had before it a photograph of a perky teen with a telephone receiver in the crook of her neck; no piercings, no roughneck clothes, hair all grown out and shiny, but Stephanie nonetheless. And when he needed to show pitiful more than innocent, he instead indicated the plumper, sadder girl seated next to his partner at the counsel table.

Once, Morrissey waved an index finger at his client and described her as, basically, a wreck of a person. "She is a pathetic young lady," he said, still pointing, "not very attractive . . . overweight."

Claire, when speaking for the defense, was very convincing about Stephanie's obedience to her fiendish friends: Not only was Stephanie their drug-runner and their round-the-clock taxi, she said, but Claire could also place them at

Stephanie's side for many of the cash withdrawals that a bank teller had earlier itemized for the court.

Claire was no angel: She faced her own charge of "accessory to murder after the fact" for helping clean up the Tempo and for failing to call the police. But in her gray knit dress and shiny flats, her newly streaked hair flipping neatly under at her shoulders, she looked trustworthy for the girlfriend of an accused murderer.

And once the jury was able to picture Claire dutifully pushing Stephanie around in a wheelchair, it was clear enough that the defendant could not possibly have negotiated that rugged murder scene in the dark.

THE WITNESS

Dana testified at Stephanie's trial too, and by now it was with a sense of dread, not just about her role in this miserable prosecution—snitch, traitor—but at her inevitable encounters with Cathy Wilson.

They were technically on the same side here: Dana was without question the star prosecution witness, responsible along with those videotaped confessions for convicting two of her good friends so far. But Cathy had come to feel that Dana was just as much to blame for Stacey's death as the others. First she had lured her to Richmond, then she had stood by and watched this brutal murder.

Was she really so ill that night, so paralyzed and witless? Cathy thought not: Dana's silence the following day, traipsing around Richmond with her daughter's killers, was proof of her collusion. And now Dana's presence every day in court was a constant reminder of the Commonwealth's refusal to prosecute her.

Tracy Bitner's reprieve the month before had finally shaken Cathy Wilson's faith in the Commonwealth attorneys. Now, at Stephanie's trial, she began to question their every move—and failure to move. Where were Stacey's rings? Where were the fingerprint reports that one expected

in high-profile murder cases like this one? The answer—
that the prosecutors already had what they needed: full confessions and the testimony of a first-hand, if addled, witness—was beside the point for Cathy. She wanted to know
what had happened to her daughter in every possible detail,
and she wanted them all put to death.

Cathy spoke her piece publicly, in comments to the press,
but it was more than evident in court as well. Sitting stiffly,
her blond hood of hair tipped back just enough to reveal
heavily lidded, bitter eyes, she was wired with rage. One
day she and some friends even muttered aloud in the courtroom about the abuse they hoped would befall the defendants in prison.

She seemed to hold her worst venom in reserve for Dana,
though, perhaps because Dana's transgressions went beyond
the legal issues now. In court, over and over again since
January, she was the one telling everybody—just stating it—
that Stacey was a lesbian, that Stacey didn't get along with
her mom, that, as Cathy saw it, up was down and down was
up.

One day in the courthouse parking lot, a red-headed
woman who had been sitting with Kathy approached Dana
with a manila folder.

"It was her birthday Sunday," the woman told her, handing over the folder and scurrying away. When Dana opened
it, she was looking at an oversized photograph of Stacey
holding up the middle finger of her right hand.

Dana took the folder to Detective Zeheb, in court most
days anyway about his own testimony. And sometimes he
escorted Dana from the courtroom, always quiet and up-
standing in a blue blazer with gold buttons and a tie.

Stephanie was found guilty of first-degree murder on March
29 and given a recommended sentence of 20 years, plus 30
days for abduction. There had been negotiations on and off
about a guilty plea, but to no avail.

And then there was one.

Turtle's case loomed under perhaps the most pressure of all. First, her capital murder verdict might be the exception to make the rule: Letting a second white girl get away without the death penalty would look very bad. But there was also the matter of her particular role in this murder. By now, the word "ringleader" stuck to Turtle like mud on a sneaker.

It was easy to cast Domica and Stephanie as disinterested members of a crew, hooked into this crime by their personalities more than the conflict itself. And while Stacey had been a thorn in Tracy's side as Turtle's other suitor, she couldn't have wanted her gone that badly if she was still with Sandy.

Hadn't Stacey been Turtle's own beef? She had injured her a lot less than some of her friends, but hadn't she provoked the whole thing in the first place?

34:

"We have a trial coming up where we have a man who hired two people to kill two businessmen in Chesterfield County. You have the two triggermen— the killers are culpable—but so is the individual who hired them to do it, because without him it wouldn't have happened, even though he didn't actually kill anybody.

"You would say that he has less blood on his hands, but we're trying to portray him to be the worst of the bunch. Because the others would not have committed the crime were it not for him and his inducements."

— Chesterfield County Deputy Commonwealth
Attorney Warren Von Schuch

Doris Tibbs was the only mom not to make the trip to the courthouse for her daughter's trial. Not that Turtle particularly wanted her there—and somebody had to watch Marisa. The courtroom's blue movie-theater–style seats filled up quickly enough on this fourth round at the Circuit Court. And Michael Hicks, Turtle's "step-dad," did attend, looking like a scared rabbit in his mussed blond beard and glasses.

Tracy's mother, Joanne Seward, was there too, tall and straight-backed, her feathered, over-the-shoulder hair painted with wide, blond stripes. Frank Winckler, Sr., sat next to her, and she tilted her head to the side sometimes to hear him whisper—discreetly, briefly, before turning his trim white whiskers back to the courtroom. If Frank Senior had been torn up by now, deeply and permanently saddened by his ravaged family, he was the rare diplomat. The kind, level man in the neat woolen blazers had won the confidence of all sides—three trials and so much discord later.

The snappy, chestnut ponytail on Joanne's left flank belonged to the other marathon spectator of the Stacey Hanna trials: 20-year-old Crystal Robinson. She had befriended all four defendants on a weekends-only grand larceny sentence at the Riverside jail and then started coming to court. Out of curiosity first, and later with such fascination that she was keeping files at home with all the newspaper clippings. She knew these girls and still couldn't believe what they had done. Her tiny girlfriend, Inky Wilson, was with her today.

"This love triangle had homosexuals, or lesbian ladies, involved," the County's chief prosecutor, Commonwealth Attorney Billy Davenport, was telling a pool of wide-eyed juror candidates. He faced them with his hands in his pockets, a tight, wrinkled pose for his squat figure, and his pinstripes cut into him. Did these Chesterfield County citizens have any problem being fair, he wanted to know, with people living that "lifestyle"?

Coming from this man, this steady, thick-haired, model of calm, you could think about a question like that and be honest about it. Not because he goaded you or, on the contrary, wanted you to keep your prejudices quiet and carry them secretly into the deliberations. Or so it seemed: The prosecution's public stance throughout the Stacey Hanna murder trials was that it was just as concerned as the defense attorneys about anti-gay attitudes among the jurors. As the argument went, it was not just the defendants but the victim too who might have her value diminished in the eyes of a bigoted jury.

Jurors trusted Davenport all the more if they had followed his rise in the county and knew him as a former steelworker, a master of commitment and wholesomeness down to the six kids and the high-school sweetheart/cheer-

leader wife. If he was not exactly one of them, he was an
accomplished and yet humble neighbor. Even now, at 50,
the suit chafed not just for his size; you could more easily
see him in the workpants of 25 years back that he had fa-
mously changed into every afternoon before making the
daily trek between law classes on the University of Richmond campus and a job setting steel at one or another con-
struction site around town.

As the elected chief prosecutor in the County for eleven
years now, with 19 lawyers working under him, he was
famous for doubling the number of jury trials—cops loved
him, they said, and that was why he was able to bring so
many cases into court. His approach to the criminals themselves was unyielding but benign and confident. No drama,
just decorum.

The star of the Turtle Tibbs defense team was in many
ways the polar opposite of the Commonwealth Attorney.
John McGarvey, a goateed, sunlamped cowboy, sauntered
around the courtroom as if he were entering a saloon after
a long ride on a horse. He had a way of leaving the room
hungry with long, open-ended pauses that were punctuated
by more slow, horsey, pointy-toed walking. Sometimes his
hands even grazed his belt where the holsters would be.

If there were questions about his handling of this case,
for he was not as slick as Joe Morrissey, no one would
dispute his devotion to the defendant and her family. He had
represented Turtle in her juvenile court case at 16 and he
was friends with Doris and helped out her current boyfriend
with his own legal problems. Out of court, he was a roughneck joker and alternated with Turtle between the roles of
senior adviser and friend.

McGarvey had a few minutes at the jury box with each
member of a whittled-down jury pool, after Billy Davenport
had finished with them. In between, he walked back to the
table that was positioned farthest away from the jury box
on the right side of the courtroom, and took a seat next to
Turtle Tibbs herself, who regularly fingered a large vertical

Band-Aid on her left temple that covered a cyst she had developed in jail.

She wore a matching blue skirt and jacket that was so loose and so burdened by shoulder pads that it looked as if a bigger person had been fitted in bed sheets and passed the outfit along. The real story was that John McGarvey had insisted absolutely on a dress, the broader the better to cover her tattoos. And so Turtle had asked her mom to go down to Kmart and pick something out. The shoes, sandals really, had crisscrossing elastic straps.

Turtle's hair was down, in another concession to the jury that didn't quite work: Hanging that way over her shoulders, it was stringy and dry, and accomplished neither femininity nor formality. The Band-Aid—her only adornment since the removal some time back of all stray loops and posts—probably did more to bring these average citizens around to her side than all the rest.

Then again, this frumpy hausfrau was no "ringleader."

On the second day of Turtle's trial, a full jury was seated— lots of parents with daughters, the attorneys noticed—and six witnesses were sworn in and sent outside to the wooden benches in the hallway. From there, it was a quick escape down the back stairs and outside if you needed to smoke. But then you had to go all the way around to the front of the building and back through the metal detector. Mostly, witnesses hovered near the courtroom door, with friends or family around them whenever possible so as to prevent any stray eye contact with someone testifying for the other side.

The cast of characters was almost the same as at the other three trials, inside the courtroom and out, except that it was harder to forget at this one that the case at hand had scooped up and shaken around an entire underground community. Turtle's trial had drawn, not more press or parents or "experts," but more teens—an extra contingent of awkwardly neatened but distinctly boyish little girls and young adults. They clung together, without touching, and looked stern in the manner of people who knew enough about this brutality stuff not to call attention to themselves.

These were not strangers, though, prompted by publicity or pity to come to a sister's side; there had been no such outpouring of anonymous gay support for any of the defendants. These were Turtle's friends, a mix of genuine confidantes and peripheral fans from her once-expansive circle.

Robyn was among them today and Monique too—although Monique was going out with Dana now. That was a little uncomfortable, but Robyn was doing well enough on her own. She'd been back from Dale City for several weeks and was making plans to move down south a ways to an old house on some underused land near Farmville that belonged to her family.

It wasn't definite yet, but Robyn was thinking about raising ostriches there. She had read all about it—a story on ostrich farmers in the *Richmond Times–Dispatch* this very day explained that ostrich meat is very low in cholesterol, and you can sell the feathers and hides, too.

Whatever Robyn decided to do in the way of starting a business down there, the land was going to make a nice weekend place for Marisa to visit. Lately the two were spending a lot of time together, and Robyn was starting to wonder about her place in the little girl's future.

Up at the front of the courtroom, Commonwealth Attorney Davenport prepared to sketch out the most complicated case of his career in the simplest terms possible. It would be rough—at the other trials, even his deliberate tongue had tripped perilously at times, confusing "Stacey" with "Tracy" and "Stephanie." He positioned a large pad of white paper on an easel in the middle of the courtroom and used a fat, black felt-tipped pen to write down eight names—the six in the car that night, plus Robyn and Claire—storytelling as he went.

The victim shoplifted the very knives that would kill her, out of love for the defendant here, he said. The killers drove past this very courthouse with their victim struggling in the trunk. And so on.

Then it was John McGarvey's turn to try out an opening argument, and with this story—this confessed story—still hanging in the air, McGarvey was not about to suggest that his client was fully innocent. The murder was something she had simply been caught up in, he said, but now she was contrite. He introduced "a tale about misfits" and quickly set about distancing Turtle from the roughneck cast of characters on Mr. Davenport's sketch pad.

"Kelley Tibbs never cut anybody, never threw a cinder block at anybody," McGarvey said. On the contrary, she tried to keep the others from carrying out these horrible acts. "She attempted to stop it to the point where she got hurt herself," he said, conjuring a lively, visual moment for the jury where, in a spray of blood, Turtle demanded, "What the fuck are you doing? Let's get out of here!"

Stacey Hanna's autopsy, McGarvey noted with a shrug, showed no signs that her body had been penetrated with a stick. This was simply a braggart's tale, conceived to keep the others from returning to that scene—perhaps designed to spare their victim's life. "Kelley was at the side of Stacey Hanna telling her she was sorry," McGarvey said. "She kicked a stick in disgust."

McGarvey now complained about Davenport's repetition of the word "lesbian," implying that he was trying to stir up any stray biases among the jury. Whether or not it was true, such a statement also served a broader purpose, by reminding the jury that the Commonwealth side might not be as pure as it seemed: The guys with the tassels on their loafers were allowed to have prejudices and the jurors were allowed to catch them.

The defense side's opening statement ended with an early but crucial nod to the petty crime that had put Turtle in sight of the death penalty. The only items taken from Stacey that didn't actually belong to Turtle were the still-absent rings. "You can't have a robbery if it's your stuff," McGarvey told the jury, dropping his chin slightly so that his cowpoke sincerity might shine over his reading glasses.

*   *   *

The entrance of Cathy Wilson, who now took a slow stroll out into the middle of the courtroom, was as dramatic as ever, but by rote now. Her eyelids looked weighted by sleepiness at first, her dark brows so flat as to be without expression. But on her first look up after the turn into the witness box, you saw the outrage burning there.

Still, it was normalcy and simplicity that Davenport was after, and Cathy delivered. Her testimony came quickly and with the grammar and intonations of the mountains. Yes, she lived in Lynchburg—"all mah life mostly."

In the months before Stacey's death, Cathy told the Commonwealth Attorney, her daughter lived right nearby: "She had an apartment but she came to mah house for meals." Though Davenport didn't mind Stacey looking like a good girl, conjuring a tight mother–daughter bond was Cathy's agenda, really—a hedge against the talk about her daughter being a lesbian and this blame coming her own way about Stacey's bad childhood.

Davenport asked about her daughter's jewelry, and she said that Stacey always wore a gold seashell pinky ring and a garnet set in gold. Then he got some details about their last conversation on the afternoon before her murder, a quick update on the plan to get her home. And he showed her a round, green watch with a brown band, and Cathy said, Oh yes, that's the one she had bought her daughter at a Florida flea market not so long ago.

On her way back to her seat, she let her eyes linger icily on Turtle's downturned head.

Cathy's friend Lisa Danner, a high-strung woman with a poof of heavily streaked hair and plastic, Sophia Loren–style glasses, was next, and you could tell from the way she licked her lip-linered mouth that she was also steaming mad. She had a story to tell about signs that Stacey was in trouble earlier that July. The trick was in not looking like she'd been sitting on her hands about it, and at the same time, to keep from getting too sad. Lisa had already been through something quite like this: Her own son had been killed four years earlier.

She told the court about first meeting Stacey in Lynchburg right after losing her son. Stacey had kept her from taking her own life, she explained. They hadn't spoken much in the last year, and she was surprised to find her here, in Richmond. Stacey had called one day and asked her to visit her at a new job at the Chesapeake Bagel Bakery, and it was the horror of that visit that had put her on alert about the scuffle on Friday, July 25th at the house.

Seated there at a polished wooden table with Richmonders contentedly licking at cream cheese all around her, it had taken Lisa a few minutes to notice the problem. Seeing Stacey was pleasant enough; she loved the way she called her "my aunt." But then it became apparent that Stacey was being held prisoner by the group of girls she now introduced.

"Girls" was the Commonwealth Attorney's own choice of vocabulary. "I guess you would call them girls . . . *animals*," Lisa growled. "She could not speak to me by herself. She always had to have somebody with her."

Following so closely on the testimony of Stacey's own aggrieved mother, Lisa might have been just the adult confirmation the Commonwealth needed to cast the teenage defendant as a brute with brutes for friends. But Lisa had also just alerted the jury that neither she nor Cathy had found Friday's beating brutish enough to follow up that Saturday with an emergency rescue.

Also, Lisa's story of Stacey's captivity was too extreme; the next witness, one of the "animals" herself, simply didn't measure up.

"What is your sexual orientation?" Davenport asked Dana Vaughan, flushed like a beet with nervousness, although not particularly about this first inquiry. It had seemed odd—immaterial even—at the first trial, but spectators had long ago stopped wincing at the question.

''I'm a lesbian,'' she answered, glancing quickly around the courtroom to see where her friends—and Cathy Wilson—were sitting.

Dana delivered the same basic murder story every time she went to court—but always with a great willingness to do what she could for the defense, especially as she came under cross-examination. Today, in her fourth time around, Cathy Wilson had reason to hate just about everything she said.

First, Dana hurt the case for capital murder by taking the sting out of the robbery: They all wore each other's things, Dana told the courtroom—and so much of it was gifts from Stacey anyway. Next, John McGarvey wanted to hear what Dana knew about that green watch that Cathy Wilson had claimed to have given her? Dana said that Stacey had shoplifted it for Turtle. And why did she think that Stacey had left Lynchburg? ''It didn't look like she was very happy,'' came the tentative answer.

Next, the court heard from Claire Watson about her next-day discoveries inside Stephanie's car, and then a couple of forensic detectives itemized their bloody finds at Marsh Field, Nash Road, and Matchpoint. A matted, stained square of grass appeared in a Polaroid photograph and a white piece of cinder block in another. Also a baseball hat with ''Sandy'' scrawled on the back, a pair of Hooters boxer shorts, a t-shirt with a big red stain under the right arm, some white corduroy shorts with blood across the front, and some shoes—including Turtle's Airwalks.

In a cross-examination of Detective Dave Higgins of the Forensic Unit, McGarvey made sure the jury understood that the eight-foot stick found at the murder scene—which he now grasped daintily in one hand like a paper wand—was so rotten as to be featherweight. The implication being that it was no weapon. McGarvey also attempted to leave the court with an impression of gross ineptitude in Higgins' department: Nobody, for example, had pulled together a decent set of fingerprints.

Detective Zeheb's visit to the stand, a rundown of his sidewalk conversations that Sunday night with both Tracy and the defendant, was a nice segue into today's key witness: Tracy Bitner.

Tracy's hair had grown out into a pair of shiny waves, parted slightly to one side. Her skin was dull and greenish but still it looked baby-soft, and Turtle also noticed that jail had made her puffier. Tracy, clean-cut and duty-bound in the same brown v-neck sweater and white t-shirt that she had worn every day to her own trial, looked up expectantly at Billy Davenport.

Did she know what kind of lies Stacey Hanna was telling that had made the others mad? Nope. Was there any reason for her to be angry at Stacey Hanna? No, sir. On the way back from Ruby Tuesday that Saturday night, who came up with the idea of kicking Stacey's butt? Tracy was not sure who started it, she said, but all four were involved.

"I don't really think there was so much of a plan," she told the Commonwealth Attorney. "It was brought up. And then it happened."

At Marsh Field, Tracy continued, she herself had grabbed one of the blades and cut Stacey with it—and Turtle's hand too, by mistake.

"But then [Stacey] was crying, she wanted us to call her mom, she was bleeding real bad.

"I thought that was enough," she said then, turning her head to the left and looking directly at Turtle, who now dropped her gaze to the fine grain of the counsel table. Later, it was Turtle and Domica who put Stacey in the trunk, Tracy said.

At Nash Road, Tracy got a razor from Stephanie, who then went back to the car. Stacey was crying and asking for her mother again and so Tracy put her hand over her mouth.

Why did she help take Stacey's clothes off? Davenport asked, and the question seemed to annoy the witness, as if she had heard it many times and still couldn't believe the plainness of the answer: "Because they were Kelley Tibbs'!" she said, almost yelling.

Turtle lowered the knuckles of her left hand from their position just over her cheek bone. The gravity of her downward stare left her hair way over her ears.

"I cut her throat," Tracy continued. "And Kelley came around and choked her, put her hands around her throat."

Now Turtle looked up in disbelief.

When court was adjourned that day, Turtle and Tracy found themselves in adjacent courthouse holding cells on the way back to their respective jails. There was a wall between them but they could talk.

"What did you say that for?" Turtle asked. She was still stunned by the choking story. "That didn't happen."

"I just kinda remember it like that. Maybe I was wrong."

"What do you mean, maybe you were wrong? This is my life, you know."

It was odd: They hadn't talked like this in all these months, taken up each deadly move and openly scrambled with the blame.

"I told you to stop and you didn't," Turtle said.

"If you had stopped me," Tracy told her, "it wouldn't have gone that far."

Turtle didn't know yet that this was Tracy's second betrayal of the week.

"Oh man, we found out that that chick Courtney and Tracy is like roomed up together and doing it," a Riverside prisoner who had traveled up to Chesterfield informed Turtle later. "Roomed up" was a slight exaggeration: They weren't sharing a cell in the crucial overnight hours. But the rest was true. It had started as a couple of awkward comments about having Turtle in common and taken off from there.

What the hell was Tracy doing with Turtle's girlfriend? After that testimony, Turtle didn't think that there was anything that could hurt her more. She vowed never to speak to Tracy again.

35:

Perhaps when the killer abducted Deborah and Fred and took them to the logging road, he had a terrifying game in store for them. He told them to take off their shoes and socks, and bound their hands behind their backs. He may have been wearing night vision goggles, which enhanced moonlight, making it possible for him to see quite well as he forced them into the woods, where he intended to track them down, one at a time.

—from *All That Remains*, by Patricia Cornwell

Patricia Cornwell was frequently in the local news, and so it was nothing special to find her there around the time of the Stacey Hanna trials. But this time the spotlight was not on Cornwell's famous personal history of ruinous spending and emotional distress—or her messy lesbian romance with a former FBI agent, who had then sent her husband to jail for trying to kill her over the affair.

All that was in the past. Now somebody was taking Cornwell to court over her work, specifically her habit of modeling fiction on the real details of real murders—mostly around Richmond. Judge Melvin R. Hughes, Jr., had decided on April 1st that the Richmond Circuit Court would allow a lawsuit about certain uncanny likenesses between her 1992 *All That Remains* and a 1989 double murder just east of Richmond. The parents of the victims in that case were claiming that Cornwell had gained illegal access to confidential autopsy reports.

Coincident with the court case, Cornwell was drawing attention to herself about an old tiff with Richmond's national celebrity of the moment: Kathleen Willey, the classy Democratic Party lady who had divided her hometown, and America too, over charges that President Clinton had groped her in the White House.

Cornwell used to be a big Democrat too, until her celebrated defection to the Republican side in the last weeks of the 1993 gubernatorial election of George Allen (clinched four years later with an unparalleled $100,000 contribution to his successor).

When Willey went on "60 Minutes" about the President in March 1997, Cornwell bitterly told local reporters about an incident five and half years earlier that still burned. Willey had trespassed on her secluded West End property to "return" a pile of the crime novelist's works, she said. There was a note too, raging about Cornwell's party defection.

Some Virginians felt that Cornwell had gotten "above her raisin'," while others read their editions with pencils just to circle all the familiar references. In either case, there was a sense around Richmond that Cornwell was not always easy to be nice to, but that one had better try for fear of ending up as a character less sympathetic than Kay Scarpetta, a.k.a. Marcella Fierro.

In person, Medical Examiner Fierro is a brusque woman, small and stern. Her remarks at the Stacey Hanna trials were delivered as if she were impatient with everyone else's failure to be as clear as she. She has a way of speaking that cuts to the chase.

"The address is not my issue," she barked during one of the earlier trials under a lawyer's pressure to compare the impact of blows dealt at Marsh Field with those at Nash Road.

"If she's underwater, cut or not cut she's gonna drown," she said at another, thankfully ending a winding, amorphous inquiry into her determination to cite a double cause of death in this case.

Her purpose at all four trials was to inventory the victim's wounds and settle some disagreements—with the guide of a detailed autopsy report and that same pile of oversized color photographs of the body, newly rinsed of dirt and blood and turned this way and that on an autopsy table at the will of a camera.

The pictures, mounted on white posterboard, were designed for the jury, so that a particular wound being described might appear to all 12 jurors at the same time in some kind of objective clarity. But the lawyers bickered over them, generally over the idea of showing a gouge that the client at hand had clearly not inflicted, and the unwieldy posterboard pile trailed along with these men up to the judge and back each time. On the way, one of the photographs might flash within view of the spectators—or the jury, or the defendant—and sometimes that didn't seem to be a mistake.

When formally introduced and described, though, each picture had to be seen up close and sometimes for several steady minutes. And John McGarvey, for one, would say that these were the most horrifying autopsy photographs in his entire career. Especially with the graphic words that went along with them in court.

At Turtle's trial, there was a picture of Stacey's back with a long, deep groove that had pulled way open because the cut was parallel to the "skin lines," as Fierro explained it; side-to-side, such a wound would have been narrower, she said. And then there was a profile shot showing a mask of bruises on Stacey's face and three slices into her neck. Turtle let her hair fall forward again during this part of the testimony and cried softly.

These were not pictures on which to convict or dismiss Turtle Tibbs, however. A wound inflicted by the end of a large stick would be telling. Or marks confirming Tracy's memory of Turtle's hands around Stacey's neck, squeezing hard enough to be construed as an effort to choke the life out of her. But no, Fierro found neither of these.

So the medical examiner's testimony now veered into analysis—damage to the body not evident in the photographs. If Turtle were to be found guilty of murder, the Commonwealth would have to show that the beating she helped with was bad enough to seriously debilitate Stacey—enough to keep her from getting out of that muddy water, for instance.

Also in that vein, the Commonwealth went for the emotional impact of knowing that Stacey had fought back.

Fierro now described Stacey's hands: The cuts and bruises on her fingers and palms that suggested a long struggle to protect herself—not just from some kind of blade but also from the solid impact of repetitive kicking and punching.

Finally, there was the matter of that zig-zag of long, shallow cuts across the top of Stacey's right leg: Were they letters? Did they spell "LIAR"? As the lone assault on Stacey Hanna's body that suggested an explanation for what had happened to her, it begged some kind of nod from science.

The medical examiner herself would not weigh in on the topic, however; this kind of thing was a jury's call. Besides, no one had accused Turtle, or any of the four, and certainly none had claimed it.

Still, it must have occurred to Dr. Fierro that the girls' silence suggested that this hadn't been done as a group—and that the perpetrator had operated in secret. By now, every other mutual accusation was out on the table.

And yet no single moment had emerged in the girls' descriptions of their long rounds through the county that night during which one of them might have had the chance. At Marsh Field, Stacey was never left alone with any of them. The letters couldn't have been cut while she was in the trunk because although that was the leg facing up, the letters read from the other side. And it was too dark on that logging road to see one's own hands, never mind writing out a word.

*   *   *

The defense called only one witness of its own in this trial:
Robyn Thirkill, neat and erect in a royal blue button-down
shirt with a white tie and slacks. McGarvey spoke to her
respectfully and in their first few exchanges it became clear
that she was there to give the jury an inside picture of someone whose athleticism and strength—not to mention charm—
had been mistaken for treachery.

Yes, she said, she and Turtle used to push tables and rugs
aside for Greco-Roman wrestling sessions. Robyn had managed the team in high school. They got pretty good but there
were some bangups.

She had a quote, too, and she remembered it with such
matter-of-fact clarity that she was entirely believable, and
you forgot for a minute about any partiality she might have
as Turtle's best friend. Robyn was just back from work that
Saturday night, she said, and sitting right there on the sofa
when she noticed Domica fingering some boxcutters and
heard her inquire of Turtle whether she thought one might
be sharper than the other. Robyn said she remembered
Turtle saying, ''We can't kill the girl,'' and then she was
excused from the witness box.

As it turned out, Judge William R. Shelton gave the Tibbs
jury the same controversial instructions as Domica's got:
There was nothing about the robbery needing to be a ''motivating factor'' for them to find her guilty of capital murder.

The judge did say, however, that if the jurors didn't think
Turtle had taken an ''immediate, active part'' in the murder
and the robbery, well then they could skip right over the
capital murder charge and find her guilty of something else:
first-degree murder or maybe felony second-degree murder.

36:

"There was some kind of a show on television about a guy who was interested in wildlife, and wildlife preservation. And he was touring zoos with Marlin Perkins or 'Wild Kingdom' or something. He was watching some Bengal tigers in a cage and they were playful and batting a ball around. They had trained them to eat out of the hand, and it was a very docile, playful, cheerful type of nurture. With baby cubs and so forth. And he was so fascinated by the Bengal tiger lifestyle that he wanted to see them in the wild.

"So he went on a backpacking tour through India and found an area where they found fresh Bengal tiger tracks. He got down off the elephant with his cameras, and he went into the reeds and he came face-to-face with a Bengal tiger that was devouring some kind of prey. And the Bengal tiger lurched forward and growled and his claws clenched, and all of a sudden he realized the strength of the animal, the frenzy of the animal, how he had killed the prey and was devouring it. He was lucky he got out with his life. All of a sudden it occurred to him that this is not the same Bengal tiger that he had seen in the zoo."
—Warren Von Schuch, Chesterfield County Deputy
Commonwealth Attorney

Warren Von Schuch is so good at prosecuting capital murder cases that less-equipped counties around Virginia summon him to handle theirs: premeditated murders, that is, that include "predicate offenses" such as robbery or rape. (Or for-hire killings, or those committed by a prisoner or against a cop or multiple victims.) He would be handling the next phase of the Turtle Tibbs trial—the sentencing phase—but only if there was a guilty verdict. His fervent wish for one clearly motivated the brilliance of the closing statement that he now gave on behalf of the Commonwealth.

Von Schuch, a handsome man who towers in the courtroom at six feet, four inches and wears the plainest aviator glasses, eschews dramatic flourishes. In capital cases, the crime is generally awful enough that, he's found, the jury wants a quiet, almost soothing voice.

So that's how he told a long story about a television show he remembered seeing on a naturalist's rude awakening to the true nature of the Bengal tiger. It took a close encounter in the wild to understand that the beast was capable of terrible violence and quite willing too, nothing like the docile feline the man had once seen playing in a cage.

The tiger was Turtle Tibbs, of course, and Von Schuch was cautioning jurors not to mistake her peacefulness in court for the innocence of a bystander.

Just because she didn't draw the most blood doesn't mean she's not a killer, he was saying. But Von Schuch was also trying to slap down any lingering stereotypes about the nonviolent nature of her gender. If this was tempered here by the defendant's non-traditional appearance and the unquestioned matter of her sexual orientation, well that was great. But he had to make sure.

Von Schuch knew about the gender issue first-hand from the Beverly Monroe case, a 1992 murder trial he prosecuted just west of Richmond in Powhatan County. Monroe, a research chemist for Philip Morris, was accused of murdering her millionaire boyfriend and disguising the crime as a suicide. Von Schuch proved, with the pattern of gunshot residue and evidence of Monroe's emotional state, that it was not a self-inflicted wound. But it was a fight to convince the jury that this highly educated mother of three was capable of killing somebody.

"The video shows the real Kelley Tibbs," Von Schuch told her Chesterfield County jury now, meaning: lying and heartless. "On this planet, have you ever seen such a lack of remorse as you saw on that videotape?"

The jury would, however, please not make the mistake of believing that Turtle's actual involvement was anything less than brutal: "All you have to do is look at her shoes," he said. "She kicked so hard there was blood on her shoes." Then there was her conduct afterwards: She stayed with Stacey's tortured, still-breathing body longer than the others, and then she went back home and fell asleep. "You can judge Kelley Tibbs by that," he said.

Von Schuch's feelings of horror were delivered, as always, in the matter-of-fact tones of a man who wants jurors to trust him as much as he wants them to be horrified. With the exception of an occasional bounce up onto the balls of his feet for emphasis, he was focused and still.

Finally, he attempted to quash any doubts that at Nash Road there had been a genuine "concert of action"—the kind of coordinated behavior that makes the getaway driver just as guilty as the guy in the 7-Eleven who shoots the salesgirl.

"Stacey Hanna was dead from the moment they picked her up from Marsh Field," Von Schuch said. The murder was "one continuing, unbroken enterprise."

John McGarvey then gave his own closing statement, a slow argument delivered while pacing the perimeters of several small, invisible circles. He said the prosecution was trying to hold Turtle responsible for the actions of Tracy and Domica with a convoluted set of legal theories. The bottom line was that Turtle inflicted no lethal violence. "There's no evidence that Kelley Tibbs cut or drowned anybody," he said—and those were the official causes of Stacey's death.

McGarvey asked the jury to consider the matter of Turtle's age, her bad upbringing, and the outsider status automatically conferred on her as a gay teen: "These are confused kids . . . they are trying to fit in a world that's not going to let them fit in.'' What Turtle did in this case is lift the lid on a Pandora's box, he said. "She didn't intend for all the evils of the world to come out.''

Also, he said, "You gotta remember that Kelley had an affair with Stacey. You may wanna whip somebody's butt. But they were lovers.''

McGarvey's mistake now was to turn his attention for a moment to Cathy Wilson, whose testimony on such topics as the origin of the watch and her daughter's sexual preferences had conflicted sharply with the stories of Stacey's Richmond peers.

He called revenge a "base motive,'' and although he never mentioned her name, it was clear that he was accusing her of lying. Cathy had endured enough without this; McGarvey lost a point to the prosecution side.

"Jurors and judges want to believe that people are telling the truth—are telling what they perceive to be the truth,'' murmured Alan Cooper, sitting there that day among the spectators to write the story for the *Richmond Times–Dispatch*. "You seldom have to kill a witness, and he certainly didn't have to kill Cathy Wilson.''

It was a long wait for the verdict. Robyn, Monique, Dana, and their gang took their time eating lunch at the McDonald's down the road, and then John McGarvey told them jokes under the huge, white columns holding up the front of the courthouse. Five hours had gone by when the red light flashed over the jury room.

When every single seat in the courtroom had been filled again, the decision could be announced: Turtle was guilty—of capital murder. Not of first-degree murder with no chance of the death penalty, like the one who had actually slit Stacey's throat. Turtle, as "ringleader,'' was possibly going to pay with her own life.

Her friends huddled in the back, stricken. Elsewhere, people looked confused and didn't seem ready to leave the courtroom yet, as if needing to know the sentence before they could get back to their lives—or back to their phones for the collect calls inevitably coming in tonight from the other defendants.

When Judge Shelton adjourned for the night, Frank Winckler and Joanne Seward stuck around until the courtroom had emptied fully into the hall. And then they walked over to try and speak with Cathy Wilson. The reporters wondered what about.

Robyn, Dana, and Monique converged on the Third Street Diner and emptied some pitchers of beer. Later, they arrived, tipsy, at Michael's Sheppard Street front door—Doris and Marisa were living there now—because Turtle was supposed to be calling.

37:

- Since 1977, about 90% of all U.S. executions have been carried out in the South. The states executing the most, in order: Texas, Florida, Virginia, Louisiana, and Georgia. Over 90% of those executed had court-appointed lawyers at their original trials.

- Of the 1,200 people formally executed in Virginia's history, over 1,000 have been black.

- The death penalty costs five to six times more than life imprisonment, according to studies in a number of states. Most costs occur at trial level. Indiana, with a smaller death row than Virginia's, estimates that it could save $5 million per year by abolishing capital punishment.

- Murder rates are lower in states that have abolished the death penalty.

- Juveniles as young as 16 at the time of the murder can be sentenced to death. Virginia also executes people who are mentally handicapped.

- Every Western democracy except the U.S. has abolished the death penalty.

- Public opinion supports alternatives to the death penalty.
  —Virginians for Alternatives to the Death Penalty (VADP)

Wayne Morgan, the dour but boyish lawyer sharing the
Turtle Tibbs case with John McGarvey, had sat silently at
Turtle's right side for three days when he was given his first
chance to speak. His bailiwick as the other half of her defense team was the fight over Turtle's redeemability. Was
she the hapless victim of a bad life, or a vicious killer?
Would it be life behind bars without parole, or lethal injection?

The sentencing portion of these trials always brought in
a new cast of characters—and lost others to the fear of
dredging up embarrassing history.

Now Michael Hicks stayed away; if his name came up
in this kind of testimony, it wouldn't be to flatter him. "Do
what you have to do," he told Morgan, as in, *Tell them how
bad we were if it helps her look less like a predator.* Krista
Evans and Bridget Phelps Mayfield, two shy girls with long,
blond hair and bangs, hoped to escape as well, but Detective
Zeheb did some coaxing out in the hall, and they both testified as scheduled about good times with Stacey back in
Lynchburg.

Krista, now 20, was only four when she first saw Stacey,
a shy tot in a dress who had just moved into the house next
door. Krista introduced herself and suggested that they play
a game, but Stacey ran around and hid behind her mother.

Krista remembered her friend's passion for softball later
on—and all those boyfriends. "She's not a lesbian," she
told the court. "She's not."

She seemed to feel burdened about making this point
well, as if saying Stacey was gay would make the murder
her own fault. Or as if Stacey might come back to life if
people just believed that she was straight.

Bridget, 18, had only known Stacey as a teen. The two
had met on the school bus in junior high; Bridget cracked
a wide smile in court when she remembered Stacey's skillful
drawings of Marvin the Martian.

Both girls knew that Stacey had had troubles at home—
especially once she admitted to her step-father's abuses and
found out there was a real father out there somewhere. But

both described a giggler who was always cracking jokes and trying to get you to laugh.

Debbie Parker was also testifying for the Commonwealth and also concerned with showing Stacey's vulnerability. But her Stacey was not quite Krista's or Bridget's. She remembered a girl who never even smiled. "I don't know if I've ever worked with a child that was emotionally, physically, sexually abused over such a long period of time," she told the courtroom.

And while the greatest trauma of Stacey's life may have been the sexual part—her step-father had started molesting her, she had told Debbie, when she was in fifth grade—her mother's influence should not be discounted.

Dr. Leigh Hagan, a psychologist engaged by the defense, now chronicled the disasters of Turtle's own first years, with an emphasis on the scarce parental guidance—and schooling. "She learned pretty quickly to say, 'I'm sick,' " he said. And Doris didn't seem to care.

Then there was her gang-rape at 12, after which she climbed through the window of her bedroom, showered, went to bed, and afterwards, tried as hard as a pregnant person can to keep it a secret. Adults were making sexual advances throughout, with one of Doris's boyfriends telling her, "All you need is a man," and another going right ahead and showing her.

Dr. Hagan estimated that Turtle now functioned at the social maturity of a 13-year-old. Not that she didn't know how to take care of business; on the contrary, he said, "She was by all reports a bit of a cheerleader."

The doctor was good, but the defense case needed a personal touch, and Sarah Franklin, the ex-girlfriend, was it. She was perfect: mature and articulate but also genuine. Her message was that Turtle had had it bad, she was still just a kid, and she was trying against all odds to get ahead—with a little help from her friends: Sarah and her family had looked for a literacy course that Turtle could take, for example, but it turned out that you had to be over 18 to go for free.

Sarah's testimony was moving—even in the eyes of the "other side." Debbie Parker found her very brave, and at one point that afternoon she approached her in the hallway to tell her so. By then the tension had built way beyond Debbie's imaginings, though; she knew that Krista and Bridget were afraid of "the lesbians" but not that the lesbians were afraid of "Stacey's people" too. When Debbie called out her name, Sarah had her back turned, and as she pivoted and saw who it was, she put her hands up in the air and cowered slightly.

"Please don't—Please don't hurt me," she whispered.

Turtle's jury decided on a sentence in just two hours, and most everybody was still at lunch. The Ukrop's grocery store cafeteria over at the Chesterfield Meadows shopping center was still crawling with lawyers and reporters. Robyn, Sarah, and Turtle's old girlfriend Melissa were finishing up at Taco Bell when Robyn's beeper went off: It flashed 911, Monique's cue from back at the courthouse that the jury was in.

As confusing and scary as the last days had been for Turtle's friends, some oddly nice things had happened between them. Watching their buddy squirm and then take a verdict of guilty had hurt. But the stress had brought down some walls—between Monique and Dana and Robyn just the night before, and now between Robyn and Sarah.

Once tense and standoffish as the best friend and the best ex-girlfriend, they were warming to each other, not just as the two who stood by Turtle but also, lately, with some of the same concerns about little Marisa's future.

Rushing out of Taco Bell, back up Route 10, and into the courthouse parking lot together, they found themselves behaving as a team. They sprinted up the stairs and down the second-floor hallway just in time. Two sets of double doors settled quietly back into place behind them and there they stood, panting in heaves, in the back right corner of the courtroom.

Judge Shelton asked the foreman to reveal the jury's decision. And there it was: life in prison. Almost everybody in the room made a small noise of some noncommittal kind.

Was this good news? It was all so confusing. People were starting to cry—except for Robyn, of course. Sarah grabbed her, though, and whatever had been between them before dissolved absolutely. "You can't pick your family," Robyn would say later.

Afterwards, asked about Turtle's sentence outside under the pillars, Cathy Wilson told a circle of reporters, "She's totally sick. She deserves to die, too."

And then, just in case anybody had missed the wild allegations inside about her daughter's lesbian leanings, she added, "My daughter was a girl. She wasn't one of them."

38:

"In the gospel of John, there is a story in which a woman is caught in adultery. In the time of Jesus, to commit adultery was one of three sins, or crimes, that was punishable by death. The other two were murder and idolatry. The scribes and pharisees were ready to stone the woman to death and asked Jesus what he thought. It was the custom that when faced with a difficult legal question, the natural and routine thing was to take the question to a rabbi for a decision. Jesus challenged those that were so ready to condemn, judge, and kill. The end result was that the crowd laid down their stones and left the woman."

—Judy Maynard, associate pastor in Richmond's
Metropolitan Community Church, hoping that
Domica Winckler's recommended death sentence
might be similarly overturned

Richmond had exactly one week before Domica's sentencing hearing to let it sink in that the two white girls got life and the one black girl got death, just enough time to get pissed off about the racism or pissed off about the charges of racism and to turn back again to the Circuit Court to see about a reprieve.

No matter that the law forbade Judge Gill from being swayed by public opinion; Domica's life was squarely in his hands. The NAACP weighed in strongly in favor of a reversal, and then on the eve of the hearing, an unlikely assortment of Domica's well-wishers filed into Richmond's bright, parkside Unitarian church to pray and consider the racial politics.

In one row, John McGarvey stood tall for the hymn-singing in a particularly nice pair of cowboy boots. In another, a young red-headed man with a goatee and an earring was sandwiched between his boyfriend and four young black children. The children's escort was "Sheryl," she told the couple when the service came around to the part where everyone was supposed to introduce themselves to somebody they didn't know yet.

Some youthful, white Unitarian ministers addressed the crowd, a racially mixed group of about 200, and there was a guitar performance. But the most impassioned of all was apple-cheeked Judy Maynard, the lesbian pastor from the Metropolitan Community Church, now crossing the dais in a clerical collar. Death row counseling was her personal beat, and this case had grabbed her right from the start.

Judy said that 1,000 of the 1,200 executed in Virginia history had been black, and then she lit into the death penalty itself: "If we continue to dispose of children like Domica, we deny the potential for redemption," she told the assemblage. "Let us all lay down our stones and let us respond with compassion."

The next afternoon, as the moment of truth approached down at the Chesterfield County Courthouse, Judy pulled together a "circle of prayer" at the top of the stairs while a royal flush of lawyers outside the courtroom stood chuckling at each other with their hands in their pockets. Besides Domica's own attorneys, Cary Bowen and Greg Carr, there was also one of Tracy's, John Boatwright, and Turtle's too, John McGarvey. Joe Morrissey was inside. On the way in, McGarvey's boots came under scrutiny from Carr, and Warren Von Schuch teased him too: "Way to go, Mr. Suntan," he said. Bowen joked with a couple of the bailiffs.

The courtroom was so crowded that Judge Gill sent the overflow back out into the corridor. All eyes were on Domica's lawyers, who paced and fussed about this precedent and that related case—and Domica herself, looking like an adolescent candidate for First Communion in a dainty white blouse with a lace collar. She rocked back and forth in her chair and sometimes when she closed her eyes to blink, her long, curving eyelashes lingered on her lower lids, as if yearning for a rest.

Greg Carr called Evan Nelson to the stand first, a forensic psychologist who struggled with a series of charts and the dense language of the social sciences to make the courtroom understand the peculiar tinderbox of teenagers traveling in groups.

People between 12 and 20 years old commit almost half of all group violence, Nelson said—for the same reason that teenagers make such good Army recruits. They're tormented by social approval, he said, and, in fact, "This is the function of adolescence—to learn to get along with peers." But it makes teens more susceptible to something called "risky shift," a sociological term from the '30s that is still the best way to describe how a group can start with a reasonable premise and end up with, say, a dead body on its collective hands after a series of small, incremental decisions.

Add some extra conformity when there are "issues about them that make it harder to fit in." Add alcohol—the only substance that the National Institutes of Health actually links to violence. And boom, you have a disaster.

Nelson didn't speak directly to Domica's own circumstances. And he had been on standby for some of the other cases too; his lecture applied to them all. But Domica was such the follower in this, so beaten-down herself, and so explosive out there with Stacey that night when she finally started lashing out, that even delivered on a chart, Nelson's take rang true all around the courtroom.

Cathy Wilson's appearance next came as a surprise to most of the spectators. There had been hints of what was to come; the reporters whispered about a warming in recent weeks. She had been seen speaking to Frank Winckler, not necessarily taking instructions but perhaps penetrating his family's humanity.

"I feel like if she was to receive death, awl of 'em

should," Cathy told a silent, stunned courtroom. She struggled for a minute to explain why, and somehow when she raised the matter of Stacey's own will—"My daughter was not prejudiced at awl"—it was heartbreaking. Not just for the benefit to Domica but also because there had been so much fighting about who Stacey Hanna had been in life. And about whether or not her mother really cared about that.

When Domica stood later and turned to speak to Cathy, now back in the spectators' box in a warm ring of friends, she could barely speak. "I just want to say, Cathy, that I'm sorry for what I did," Domica said, and the rest was lost in a flutter of sobs.

Moments later, Judge Gill announced that he would be reversing the jury's recommendation. Pam Winckler smiled and looked straight up at the ceiling of the courtroom, and Domica stopped rocking.

That spring and summer, charges against Claire were dropped and the other sentences were confirmed: Stephanie would do 20 years, and the three would do life, with a first chance at release when they turned 60.

Nobody was getting the death penalty after all—and, in retrospect, it might be argued that this was by sheer luck.

Some people in Richmond and Chesterfield County said that there had never really been a chance that any of them would end up on death row. They just don't do that to girls, they said.

Political will is one thing, and it may be true that Chesterfield County wouldn't have permitted such a spectacle—although the explanation would just as likely be their age as their gender.

But the legal facts, at least, suggest that all three of the original capital candidates would have gotten the death penalty if it weren't for Judge Daffron's very specific instructions to Tracy's jury about the robbery needing to be a direct motivation.

The argument goes like this: When Tracy testified at Turtle's trial, those jurors learned as a matter of course that she hadn't gotten death herself—and so they certainly couldn't give it to the girl who had done less. And there was no way that Domica was getting lethal injection on her own, whatever the color of her skin.

PART EIGHT

Stations of the Cross

"We see an increase in violence as young people come out at younger ages. They feel they've been a victim of society and they take it out on other youth."

—Rea Carey, National Youth Advocacy Coalition

39:

"When I heard testimony that Stacey was calling for her mother, it took my breath away. I went, 'Oh Jesus.' But that's the way they were: 'We can treat each other like shit, but nobody else is going to treat us like shit.' "

—Debbie Parker

Brookville High School is a low, brick building alongside Route 460, the four-lane highway that connects old Lynchburg with the dizzying mall creep on its southern side. At the end of July 1998, a year after the murder of a former Brookville student named Stacey Hanna, classrooms stood empty all up and down the corridors; the low-gear activities of summer kept one front office barely going. A sign out at the grassy edge of the highway advertised "Cheerleaders Car Wash, Saturday 9–3. Ain't it nifty!"

Heading farther south on 460, Campbell County becomes Bedford County, the main jurisdiction for the case that Stacey had hoped to file against her stepfather. The years of her abuse also included incidents in Campbell County and Lynchburg itself, as the family moved around from one house to another. But it was the connection that Stacey had made with the Bedford County Department of Social Services—in the person of Debbie Parker—that had endured, all the way into the Chesterfield County Circuit Court and even now as Cathy Wilson carried on with the perpetually unfinished business of finding justice for Stacey's murder.

The anniversary of the murder was coming up when Cathy paid her first call to Debbie's busy basement office in months. Back before the trials, Cathy had taken Debbie for an ally: Debbie would tell everybody in court how difficult Stacey had been, she figured; she would set the record straight that Cathy was not to be blamed for any of her daughter's troubles.

It wasn't that simple. But neither was it as simple as Debbie's blunt comments in court—physical and emotional abuse? That was pure lies, as Cathy saw it.

Today, sitting across from Debbie at the same pale desktop where Stacey had so often rested her tired head, Cathy told her just that. And how the disappointments of these trials had sent her furiously in search of something more powerful, something better fitting the cruelty of this crime than the long and cushy lives that these girls would now enjoy in prison. She wouldn't rest, she told Debbie, until Tracy, Turtle, and Dana all got the death penalty.

Debbie's instinct was to use textbook counseling tools to help Cathy with her pain, to coax her into *accepting* that Stacey may have been angry with her for failing to protect her from her stepfather—and for who knows what other, more-benign teenage complaints, such as making her babysit her little brothers all the time? But Debbie hesitated and switched gears entirely: Not only wasn't it her job to counsel Cathy, it wasn't likely she'd listen.

"I testified to what was in my file, which was what your daughter told me," Debbie finally said.

A file, though, that Cathy could now never see—it had been destroyed ten months earlier, under a law governing minors in cases never formally opened.

Neither Lynchburg nor Bedford County was a likely hiding place for the answers that Cathy was looking for, and so she headed back to the eastern part of the state: The next stop on her whirlwind, get-to-the-bottom campaign was none other than Riverside Regional Jail. One day, there she was on the other side of the glass in that boxy visitors' room—to see Domica. She wanted Stacey's rings. Where had Domica hidden the rings?

The question—the visit—was not entirely a surprise. Cathy had been in touch with Domica's grandfather. But Cathy wanted to ask Domica herself, and it worked. Domica phoned Frank with the details about where to find them, and he gave Cathy that pinky ring and that gold band with the pretty garnet setting.

There was speculation about a spoken or unspoken *quid pro quo*: Is this why Cathy had helped Domica escape the death penalty?

In any case, Cathy's obsession with the jewelry had little to do with having Stacey's scattered personal possessions to hold, as meaningful as that may have been. Cathy stormed into Billy Davenport's office on August 12th, the same day that Stephanie's 20-year sentence was confirmed, and let it rip. Warren Von Schuch was there for part of it, just enough to get the gist of her blustery speech.

"How come I had to go and do this?" she wanted to know.

Meaning: What kind of lousy case did you mount that I had to be the one to find the stolen goods? And by the way, how come you still won't indict Dana?

The attorneys pointed out, not for the first time, that they had put three young ladies away for life—and hadn't needed the rings in hand to do that. And then they jousted back: Dana wasn't the only one going unprosecuted; Cathy herself had avoided charges of felony obstruction of justice. It was she, they suggested, who had enlarged that photograph of Stacey presenting her middle finger and had it handed to Dana Vaughan by that red-headed lady in the courthouse parking lot.

"Well, you can't prove that," Cathy told them.

Von Schuch, used to grateful, even fawning behavior from victims' families, was at the end of his rope with this woman.

"Yes we can," he told her.

Cathy now told them both, "Fuck you" and later noted

ominously on television that Davenport wouldn't be in office forever.

She was a tangle of misdirected rage. But certainly it was a proper complaint: Recovering that watch from Domica on the night of the arrests would have given the police probable cause to search her home for the rings. And the taking of those rings from Stacey amounted to the only *genuine* thievery—the only *genuine* factor to kick those charges up to capital murder.

Cathy was perhaps fortunate that the juries hadn't minded.

As for her charge that the Commonwealth Attorney's Office, up there counting its capital convictions and then moving on, didn't care about this case as much as she, well that was certainly true. But who possibly could?

40:

The Commonwealth of Virginia was building prisons like crazy in the mid-1990s, but not for women, even though the need was growing several times faster than it was for men. And even though, in the hand-me-down facilities devoted to women, things were generally worse—not just crowded, but inferior. In one year alone, at one women's prison alone, an inmate bled to death, another was diagnosed with terminal ovarian cancer after months of unattended abdominal pain, and still another hanged herself.

Enter Fluvanna Women's Correctional Center, a small city of beige buildings with green roofs on 30 acres about an hour and a quarter northwest of Richmond. When its state-of-the-art electronic fences hummed to life for the first time in May 1998, Fluvanna's idealistic young warden promised top-of-the-line health care and extra consideration to job training and substance abuse and parenting—plus the women would not be treated like animals. And this was not just to be nice, she said, or to win high marks from prisoners' rights groups, but to cut down on the risk of escape while transporting the women outside on emergencies.

Fluvanna had beds for 1,200, but the warden hoped to start out with 900—if she could just keep the staff. In the prison's first months, there were rumors of a swift turnover among the guards: Veteran employees of the prison system chafed under the new-fangled regime: Trying out kindness on so many hundreds of murderers and thieves was easier said than done. The staff was further deluged by a multitude of transfers from Iowa (Virginia rented out cells all over the state to make up for the overbuilding).

*   *   *

Friends of Incarcerated Women and the ACLU would wait
and see; they were going to give Fluvanna a few months
to get its prison in order. But the news making it into
Riverside Regional Jail was only good. And by now it
looked like that's where all four of Stacey Hanna's killers
were going.

It was mostly the contact visits and the schooling and the
paid jobs that the four craved, and all of that was standard
prison policy. But a stray Fluvanna canteen receipt or a ru-
mor about comforters on the beds or ovens that turned out
fresh bread every day of the week was enough to fuel wild
flights of fantasy about the long years ahead.

"It's kinda like being on a college campus except you
can't leave," Stephanie guessed from the stories she had
collected. She pictured herself toting books across a vast,
scholarly hall in a Nine Inch Nails t-shirt from home. Even
if it was all talk, she reasoned, it had to be more interesting
than sitting around Riverside sorting the stickers that her
mom had mailed her and dyeing her now–fully unpigmented
hair pale pink with packets of fruit punch Kool-aid.

Turtle dreamed too. Contact visits with Marisa would be
the main thing, but she would also need a new look. As
soon as she got settled in, she was going to start twisting
her hair into dreadlocks. She'd have to wait, though, or
they'd shave it off; people lost all manner of braids and
weaves and clumps in the anti-lice routine on the way into
the DOC—the state Department of Corrections system.

Tracy was the first of the four to actually make the transi-
tion, but there would be no reporting back about the bed-
clothes or the bread or the rules about hair. Tracy wanted
nothing to do with any of her old friends, as she told Turtle
regularly via a third party—Courtney, ex-girlfriend of both,
now serving her own sentence over at Goochland and writing to both of them.

"Tracy put a Keep Separate on you so if you do go to

Fluvanna, you won't be together," Courtney informed Turtle by mail. Also, "Tracy hates you. She doesn't want you to ever write her again."

"Why can't Tracy write me and tell me this herself?" Turtle would inquire in the next letter.

"Because she doesn't want to have any contact with you. Because she knows if she writes you, you're going to write her back."

Turtle always had to wonder how much of this was Courtney's own agenda, whatever that might be in this odd new triangle of theirs. But that summer they wrote each other almost every day, sometimes filling up as many as twelve pages, front and back, with the subject of Tracy holding at a steady page or so.

Communicating with Domica didn't have the same urgency, the same love/hate compulsion that kept the former lovers always still a little bit in touch. But Domica had started out as the quiet one and by now had left the others high and dry for so many months that the news that began surfacing through intermediaries was snatched right up.

A young inmate named Wednesday introduced herself to Turtle as Domica's "girlfriend" and seemed to mean just that. And later, when Domica left for Fluvanna, there was Melissa, who was moved to tell Turtle some things that she hadn't dared say until Domica was out of sight.

"Mica loves you," Melissa told Turtle. "She cares about you a lot. And this whole thing has fucked all o' y'all up."

Domica had cried the day of Turtle's sentencing, Melissa said. And when the *Richmond Times–Dispatch* arrived in the pod the next morning and some of the women were looking it over, Domica had grabbed it away, insisting that they just didn't understand: They didn't know Turtle Tibbs.

Melissa urged Turtle, "Write her. She'll write you back. It's just a bunch of bullshit that got fucked up. And, you know, y'all got a lotta shit to get straight, but y'all are friends."

*   *   *

There was no better agent of communication, though, than shaved-headed, 18-year-old Adrian. With all the time that the four had spent at Riverside and all the pod switching, everyone but Domica got to know her. Adrian had befriended first Tracy, then Turtle, then Stephanie.

Sometimes it was quite on purpose that one dispatched comments via Adrian to another, sometimes not. Stephanie would have preferred not to know, for example, that Tracy was telling people that Stephanie had been the one to carve "LIAR" on Stacey's leg. What a load of shit, she fumed. But hey, they were all Adrian's friends.

Sparing the poor girl the manipulations of this gang was, of course, impossible: Turtle insisted that Stephanie's latest Keep Separate was to keep Turtle away from Adrian, for example. But the benefit of all this time spent at the middle was that no one at Riverside could match Adrian's insight into the frailties and manipulations of the Triangle girls.

"You still love her," Adrian told Turtle about Tracy, now off in prison but maybe one day in her life again.

"I don't!"

"If she were to walk in the door right now, you would be down on your knees."

"I would not!"

Turtle knew, of course, that it was true. She had less of an idea what they would talk about or ask each other at such an impromptu meeting, although she had some ideas.

Why had Tracy, for starters, pushed with such a fury that night to turn their "ass-whipping" into something more— directing them down darkened country roads like that and manipulating Stacey's body so far into the dark that there had been no choice but to keep beating her? And why had Tracy testified against Turtle?

Then again, Tracy might ask Turtle a few things too. Why had Turtle continued to bellow her own complaint at Stacey—in words and blows, both—if what she really wanted was to put a stop to the "fury"? And why had she led Stacey on like that in the first place? Again and again, so that the girl had stopped believing Turtle's refusals?

Maybe they would talk for a while and get something resolved. On the other hand, maybe they wouldn't want to talk about it at all.

Time had intervened, and a year in the life of a teenager is a long time: enough for a size of clothes or even a whole new personality. Perhaps there was nothing in the details of their court cases or their memories of the murder itself that still needed discussion. In the same way that the passing of the anniversary had summoned back the monstrous, four-way friction of July 27, 1997 but had to be endured alone.

It wasn't just a matter of "putting it behind them," although they leapt at the chance to do that as quickly as anyone. It was that in the course of their encounter with the criminal justice system, the four had become murder "charges." Prison would determine the adults they would be, more in some ways even than the murder itself.

In fact, their actions of that night had become removed from everything but their dreams. By now each had almost entirely passed off responsibility for the murder—Turtle to Tracy's hypnotic draw; Tracy to Turtle's girl-craziness; and the other two, as dutiful soldiers in someone else's war, to anyone but themselves.

Perpetrators of more deliberate murders have some kind of "intention" to acknowledge, and still more of one if they act alone. Instead, the daily details of these four jailhouse lives simply filled the spaces where the reflection might have been.

Turtle and Stephanie stayed on at Riverside for months after the other two left, and they became obsessed with leaving, generally showing their annoyance with the delay by tangling with the jail authorities. Over a guard's insistence, for example, that a photocopy of a photograph that Turtle carried with her to GED class one day counted as a note—and could therefore be taken from her. But then, no, that it counted as a photograph. Which maybe was worse, because that meant the pile of pictures in her cell exceeded the allowance.

Then Stephanie and some of her podmates got caught giving each other hickeys. They'd been doing it for months, and though it was with barely a trace of lust, hickeys most definitely counted as "sexual misconduct," punishable by a 15-day "lockdown."

Stephanie got that plus an extra charge for the piece of cardboard with cologne on it that her grandmother had mailed in so that she could slide it into her skin cream for a perfumed scent. Nope: against the rules. So were the coloring books she was caught with—although they knocked that part off the record at the last minute.

Before she was locked in for the duration, guards stripped her cell quite bare: Out went all the paper items she had collected and the shoebox full of toys and pencils.

Being left alone in a cell for an extended period of time is standard punishment in county jails and prisons too. It wasn't necessarily a bad idea for somebody like Turtle. "I read 160 pages of this book today," Turtle told Robyn, Sarah, and Marisa one day that summer when she emerged from her own stint in isolation. Robyn's jaw went slack at the news. "And I twiddled my thumbs and I did some sit-ups," Turtle added.

Stephanie, on the other hand, was terrified of being alone. And after her first week in lockdown from the hickey bust, she was already getting panicky. Her speech over the telephone became slurred and she lost track easily of her conversations with Claire.

But some of the guards felt that Stephanie's punishment was a long time coming. Stephanie's little-girl routine was infuriating by now; they were fed up with all the stickers and paraphernalia from home, not to mention all the baby-sister treatment the other inmates seemed so glad to bestow. Stephanie was lately collecting extra chocolate milks from her doting elders and even getting her mom to help out her preferred friends with extras and snacks.

41:

"When she wrote last, she was really sweet. She said she loved me and missed me and come see her. But, damn, Fluvanna is like an hour away, and I hardly have time to see my little brother or family. I really feel guilty and I know she hates me right now. She's like that. She really is. She loves you to death but if you don't write her she wants to disown you."

—Karla

Short-term prisoners befriended or romanced along the way never seemed to measure up to the demands of anyone behind bars for the duration—and it riled these four as much as the rest. It seemed like, having spent time themselves on the inside, ex-cons would know what it meant to get a card or a phone number. Instead they disappeared into the world out there like distracted strangers, one by one, without a trace.

Even when they wrote, they always managed to fall short.

One former Riverside sweetie sent Turtle $150 in the mail with a card saying, "I love you" and "I miss you." Turtle needed the money, and the message was as nice as any. And yet it drove her crazy.

"That's pretty shitty," Turtle sniffed. "I totally felt like I was used and abused. It's like she paid me off."

Likewise, the Triangle girls were taken aback when their families and friends from the outside didn't make a routine out of keeping in touch.

The appeal of contact visits hadn't lured visitors up to

Fluvanna at quite the rate that Tracy, for example, had hoped. Her family came to see her, and hugging her little brother was worth 10 letters from Courtney. But visits and notes from Sandy and the twins became rare.

Karla was really busy at work, and Sandy hurt herself badly while totaling her truck. She'd broken her pelvic bone and the pain was unbearable. She couldn't work at all—and had to give up her Matchpoint apartment entirely. No way she was driving all the way up to Fluvanna.

There were rare exceptions to this fadeout. Robyn stopped by whenever she could, and did better than that by spending more and more time with Marisa. And Claire, lately transformed from her mannerly former self into a punkish imp with crayon-yellow hair and rainbow rings on a loop around her neck, was still and forever Stephanie's girlfriend.

Dana was also starting to come by Riverside a lot as the summer wore on. She and Stephanie had gotten friendly— but at some point, it wasn't just Stephanie she was coming to see: Dana had developed a relationship through several layers of glass with little Adrian. They were "dating" now.

"That goes to show you that they have something real," in Stephanie's opinion, " 'cause they really care about each other."

Sadly, Dana could not possibly have had room in her heart for much more than guilt. The blushing, ashamed truth-teller in court, she would always be seen—and probably always see herself—as the one who talked. Not to mention the only one in the car that night who could walk freely back out to the jail parking lot and drive away at the end of visiting hours.

In either case, whether it was love or guilt, Dana came to Riverside not so much for Stephanie as for her own purposes. Who knew if she would be making the trip all the way out to Fluvanna if Adrian wasn't there too?

*   *   *

It looked like jail itself was the only reliable source of friendship for teenagers such as these looking at an entire life in prison—so long a stretch of time that Marisa, for instance, would be 47 when Turtle had her first chance of getting out.

Turtle, not surprisingly, was adept at pulling together just the small society she needed: a circle of friends who were not just around her age but also staying behind bars for a while.

As summer turned into fall at Riverside, she became part of a tight little five-girl clique with echoes of the South Belmont crowd: Turtle, Janie, Melissa, Chantel, and Jay were among the youngest in there. Melissa, in for robbery, was the most junior at 17; she had been tried and convicted as an adult.

They became known as "The Young and the Restless" and felt compelled to fulfill everybody else's expectations of bratty behavior. One day Chantel did something nice for Melissa, for example, and Turtle got jealous:

"Oh, you love her more now than you love me? Okay, bitch. All right."

But then Chantel's feelings were hurt: "You really called me a bitch?"

"Yeah, I'm fuckin' serious," Turtle told her right back.

This sent Chantel storming upstairs to her cell, where she shut the door behind her. Turtle followed with a soft, apologetic "Don't be mad at me." And then Janie got mad because of all the arguing, and then Melissa too because nobody was watching TV with her.

42:

"I don't see her as any type of monster. She's still my best friend. And I'm going to help her out in any way I can. Just be there for her and so on.

"I feel like she got caught up. She did something stupid. That's how I feel about it, basically. She did something stupid and now she's gotta pay for it.

"I can't tell her what to do. If I did she'd probably listen to me, but I didn't want to be that type of person. I didn't want to be her dad."

—Robyn

The first anniversary of Stacey's murder was just days away when Robyn and Monique stopped by Babe's in Monique's truck. Sheba the python was with them—in a pillowcase. It was a Friday night and they were amused to find that line-dancing had not gone out of fashion since they were last in for a beer. A cluster of older men and women in khakis and pale jeans moseyed around solemnly on the bare linoleum floor in back, dodging a lone square pillar, a contented grid of sneakers and cowboy boots cavorting under a motionless disco ball.

"There's a reason . . . for the warm, sweet nights," the Bellamy Brothers twanged over the sound system as Robyn and Monique slid into a booth in the carpeted, orangey part of the bar. "There's a reason . . . for the candlelight."

It was nothing at all like New Year's—people were nice again. Like Babe's in the early days, when Robyn was the new dyke around town, rampaging with Turtle, sitting still

for the elaborate double women's symbol that now decorated her right arm. There were lots of the same faces: Vicki
behind the counter, for instance, still running things. The
same old neon beer signs plugged Budweiser and Coors,
although now there were "microbrews" on tap too. Robyn
and Monique would each have a bottle of Icehouse, please.

Some things had stayed in place and others had come
back around: Monique and Robyn were together again. And
now they were in the first stages of making the move to that
land down near Farmville. Robyn was clearing away brush
and putting a new coat of paint on the old house, and most
nights, Monique commuted the hour or so from her computer job in Richmond.

Doris planned to dispatch Marisa south at least once before first grade started in September, but meanwhile, visits
happened in Richmond. Robyn and Monique would come
by the Sheppard Street house and take her out to fly a kite
or go for a swim.

At the end of July, Robyn and Monique took Marisa
down to the river, along with Candy—Turtle's latest girlfriend, fresh out of jail—and Candy's little boy. Marisa was
dressed entirely in pink, from headband to mules, a round,
six-year-old cherub crossing delicately over a creaky, swinging rail bridge and down a winding stair.

The group foraged for a path through the woods and
emerged at a small beach called North Bank, a shady patch
of shore where the current was gentle and you could wade
way out through the exposed roots of water willows and
river birches. Rubber rafts full of day trippers floated right-
to-left on the other side of the river; the turbulent waters
up- and downstream were just a distant roar from here.

The first thing anybody had to say about Marisa was that
she was just like Turtle: charismatic, and tenacious as hell.
And also built like a truck, if a lot less prone to tomboy
fashion. She was no dummy either.

For example, Marisa wasn't supposed to know that her
mother had helped kill someone—and she was definitely not
supposed to tell Turtle that she had gone to court herself to

testify against a longtime family friend who had molested her. But she was as absorbent and as loudmouthed as any six-year-old.

"The girl that Tracy and Mama got in a fight with, she's dead," she told Sarah Franklin one day. "And they're in trouble. And I know how to talk to the judge. Now I can go tell the judge and my mom can get out."

Sarah was speechless.

Another day, Marisa was on the phone with Turtle and decided that she was annoyed about her mom being away so long. "Oh this isn't fair," she told her. "How come my trial is over with and yours isn't?"

"What? Put your granny on the phone."

By late summer, Doris was in poor health; she was in and out of the hospital with throat cancer treatments. The question begged: What if she were incapacitated for weeks or months? Counting on her current boyfriend and his sister and other patchwork babysitter arrangements wasn't a good long-term solution. If Doris got sick enough to die, custody might go to the state.

After Marisa's first few excursions with Robyn, there was talk about setting up an "entrustment," so that she could make hospital decisions if she took the kid away for the summer or even just down to Farmville on weekends. But pretty soon, with Turtle away for no less than the rest of her life, the discussion had moved to guardianship.

Robyn insisted that she was ready: She and Monique could take Marisa on full-time if they had to, or maybe in some kind of sharing arrangement with Sarah Franklin.

Robyn had seen the difference when Marisa got some basic discipline, went to bed before midnight. Lately, Marisa was cutting her own hair into a raggedy mess and nobody over at Sheppard Street was stopping her. Who was going to sit down with her at homework time?

As the guardianship discussion got serious, though, it was hard not to wonder about legal objections to this particular kind of alternative family: In Virginia in 1998, gay candidates for adoption inevitably looked to a seven-year pattern of court rulings against a woman named Sharon Bottoms, who had lost custody of her son to her mother—purely because Sharon was a lesbian and her mother was not. Even the Virginia Supreme Court had approved this at one point. Just that March, the original judge in the case had defied the Court of Appeals and ruled that Bottoms and her son would have no contact at all.

The Bottoms case had stirred up some ill will around the state. "If we were just gonna go up to an adoption agency and adopt, me and Monique and Sarah," Robyn guessed, "they'd be like, 'Hell no.' "

The gay issue would most likely kick in if Marisa's blood relatives objected to this match—and so Turtle checked with her mother from time to time on that subject. "You have to do what's best for her," she told Doris once over the phone. "I don't want her to grow up like I did."

Robyn's interest in taking over with Marisa wasn't surprising to people who knew about her devotion to Turtle. But there were inevitable comparisons with Robyn's earlier efforts to play guardian to Marisa's own mother—down to the river swims and the dream that setting up house with Robyn would set the six-year-old straight.

In the summer of 1998, the murder was still not quite explained. Not by Stacey's behavior in the hours leading up to it, not by her killers' frustration with their powerlessness in the world as poor, uneducated, gay kids, not even by what the experts had to say about what happens when you put a bunch of drunken teenagers together with a score to settle.

Some simply closed the sorry book at the point of realizing that; Cathy Wilson pushed for a payback that would never come; and Robyn chose to put some of it onto herself.

"I could have been more of a parent," she said of her "butch brother" one day on her way over to pick up Marisa for a Riverside visit. "I let her move in with the intention of helping her become a responsible adult. So when the end result is this, I can only think that I didn't help her so much.''

As for Marisa, ''When she's at our house, she's a perfect angel. It's just that her grandmother lets her get away with murder, so she does.''

43:

A neighbor up the street from Marsh Field was looking for a buyer for his house in the summer of 1998, and one day he phoned Walter Marsh with a complaint.

"Well, I can't sell the house if 'a popular drinking spot' is down there," the neighbor told him.

Walter could see his point, but rather than start again from scratch with his sign, he managed to cover up that particular offending line with a metal strip—easy enough to remove later on.

"It'll probably come off in another year when the whole murder thing is gone away," he told Charlotte.

Cathy Wilson was asked to take down that cross from alongside Nash Road at around the same time. The request came from the folks over at The Highlands, who were about to bulldoze the logging road and proceed with building homes there.

And so she drove up there one day, rocked the white plywood base loose from its earthen slot, and carried the cross back to her car. She'd keep it at home in Lynchburg for a while, give The Highlands a chance to fill these woods with people. And then she would return and see what exactly ended up there—whose living room had been constructed on top or whose lawn seed was taking root.

She would approach the new residents at home, tell them about Stacey, and inquire about putting the cross back up. That is, if she could find the spot where her daughter's body had been found without the row of pines and the gravel trail to guide her.

EPILOGUE

At 4:30 a.m. on November 18, 1998, Stephanie and Turtle were dispatched, as expected, to the Fluvanna Women's Correctional Center. It turned out that there was no such thing as Keep Separates at Fluvanna—at least not by a prisoner's personal prerogative. This raised vague fears back in Richmond that the special chemistry of 16 months back might flare again. "They've certainly shown that when they get together, bad things can happen," Greg Carr, Domica's lawyer, pointed out.

The four prisoners themselves were more concerned that their co-defendants would talk behind their backs and sabotage their own crucial efforts to get in good, especially with the precious minority of women settling into Fluvanna for the long haul.

It wasn't clear just yet what they would say to each other. The first week, Turtle, Domica, and Stephanie greeted each other in the visiting area; Domica made a special trip across the room to see Marisa. Tracy was still nowhere in sight.

A HANDSOME OVERACHIEVER AND A BEAUTIFUL
HONORS STUDENT MADE THE ULTIMATE LOVE PACT...
MURDER.

BLIND LOVE

THE TRUE STORY OF THE TEXAS CADET MURDERS

PETER MEYER
Author of The Yale Murder

Nothing could come between high school sweethearts
Diane Zamora and David Graham—but something did:
beautiful blonde sophomore Adrianne Jones. After she and
Graham had a sexual encounter, a tearful Graham confessed everything to Zamora. Enraged and out-of-control,
Diane Zamora insisted that there was only one way to
restore the "purity" of their love...so together they murdered Adrianne in an isolated spot outside of their hometown of Mansfield, Texas. There were no suspects in the
murder until months later, when Diane confessed the crime
to her military school roommates, shocking friends, family, and a picturesque Texas town...

"AN INVALUABLE BOOK FOR ANYONE WHO WANTS TO UNDERSTAND SERIAL MURDER."

—Joseph Wambaugh

WHOEVER FIGHTS MONSTERS

My Twenty Years Tracking Serial Killers for the FBI

ROBERT K. RESSLER & TOM SHACHTMAN

He coined the phrase "serial killer", he advised Thomas Harris on *The Silence of the Lambs*, he has gone where no else has dared to go: inside the minds of the 20th century's most prolific serial killers. From Charles Manson to Edmund Kemper, follow former FBI agent Robert K. Ressler's ingenious trail from the scene of the crime to the brain of a killer in this fascinating true crime classic.

"THE REAL THING. ABSOLUTELY MESMERIZING."
—Anne Rule, author of *Small Sacrifices*

WHOEVER FIGHTS MONSTERS
Robert K. Ressler
___95044-6 $6.50 U.S./$8.50 CAN.